"My friend O. S. Hawkins has written a powerful book this year that I pray will impact all who desire to see people come to salvation in Christ Jesus. Each generation has the God-given privilege of casting and drawing the net to those who hear the call of the Holy Spirit (cf. Matt 4:19). O. S. and Matt Queen masterfully shine a light on Scripture where God's servants have effectively called people to the foot of the cross. My prayer is that preachers, and all followers of Christ, will read this book with open hearts to the importance of *The Gospel Invitation*."

—FRANKLIN GRAHAM, president and CEO, Billy Graham
Evangelistic Association and Samaritan's Purse

"Every pastor, preacher, teacher, and anyone serious about sharing the gospel must read *The Gospel Invitation*. From the historical validity of the invitation to practical steps for modern invitations, you will be inspired and encouraged to invite more and more to come to Jesus."

—RYAN FONTENOT, founder and lead
evangelist, R.A.G.E. Ministries

"Every pastor I know truly wants to see people discover a relationship with Christ, and this book gives you an incredible opportunity to do that. Whether you have been extending an invitation at the end of your sermons for years or you are looking at doing it for the first time, O. S. Hawkins and Matt Queen have compiled a great resource. If you put into practice the principles and suggestions you find here, I am convinced you will see an increase in the number of people who respond to the gospel in your church."

—KEVIN EZELL, president, North
American Mission Board, SBC

T0008298

"One of the most frequent questions I receive from young leaders and communicators is: 'How do you give a gospel invitation?' I can't think of two more qualified leaders to write on this relevant and needed topic than my friends Dr. O. S. Hawkins and Dr. Matt Queen. Please get this book and share it with every leader you know. That is what I plan on doing!"

—SHANE PRUITT, National Next Gen Director, North American Mission Board (NAMB), author of *Calling Out the Called*

"The Gospel Invitation is a book begging to be read and practiced! May God use this important message to equip a new generation of preachers and evangelists to bring multitudes into the family of God."

—DR. JACK GRAHAM, senior pastor, Prestonwood Baptist Church

"The most exciting time of our worship service each week is when we give people an opportunity to publicly respond to the teaching and preaching of God's word by receiving Jesus into their life. As a pastor, I can't think of a greater privilege and more sacred responsibility. In *The Gospel Invitation*, Hawkins and Queen do an incredible job of exploring the biblical basis for a public invitation and give practical helps on how we can be most effective in calling people to Christ. You'll be a better witness for reading this book and implementing its instructions."

—JARRETT STEPHENS, pastor, Champion Forest Baptist Church, author, *The Always God: He Hasn't Changed and You Are Not Forgotten*

THE
GOSPEL
INVITATION

WHY PUBLICLY INVITING

PEOPLE TO RECEIVE CHRIST

STILL MATTERS

O. S. HAWKINS
MATT QUEEN

THOMAS NELSON

Since 1798

THOMAS NELSON

The Gospel Invitation
© 2023 Dr. O. S. Hawkins and Matt Queen

Published in Nashville, Tennessee, by Thomas Nelson. Thomas Nelson is a registered trademark of HarperCollins Christian Publishing, Inc.

Thomas Nelson titles may be purchased in bulk for educational, business, fundraising, or sales promotional use. For information, please e-mail SpecialMarkets@ThomasNelson.com.

ISBN 978-0-310-14193-8 (softcover)
ISBN 978-0-310-14214-0 (audiobook)
ISBN 978-0-310-14194-5 (ebook)

Cover design: Tammy Johnson
Cover art: © Marylia / Shutterstock
Interior design: Sara Colley

Printed in the United States of America

23 24 25 26 27 28 29 30 /TRM/ 12 11 10 9 8 7 6 5 4 3 2 1

This book is dedicated to each of the multiplied thousands of men and women, teenagers, and boys and girls over the decades of our preaching ministries who made public confessions of their faith when, "with many other words," we were privileged to offer Christ's own free invitation of the gospel.

CONTENTS

PREFACE

"I AM GOING TO ASK YOU TO LEAVE YOUR SEAT, STEP INTO the nearest aisle, and come and stand with me here at the front." Those exact words rolled from the lips of the legendary evangelist Billy Graham on thousands of occasions over six decades of public ministry. As the massive crusade choir would begin to sing, "Just as I am . . . I come, I come," millions of people across the years responded publicly and unashamedly to Christ's invitation offered by this one solitary man.

A public pledge of our personal faith helps us seal the decision in our own hearts. After all, Jesus promised, "So everyone who acknowledges me before men, I also will acknowledge before my Father who is in heaven" (Matt 10:32). When you come publicly and unashamedly to make a confession of your faith in Christ, at that moment Jesus, who is seated at the right hand of the Father in heaven, turns to His Father and with His lips forms the syllables of your name and speaks them to the Father.

The public gospel invitation has been a part of gospel preaching in the church since the very day the church was born on Pentecost after Jesus's resurrection. Simon Peter stood before the gathered throng on the Temple Mount and preached the good news—that Jesus lived, died, was buried, and was raised from the dead—and subsequently called on his hearers to repent and believe the gospel (Acts 2:14–40). Peter did not simply preach his sermon, hear a few "Amens!" and dismiss the crowd to think about it. Rather, when he had built his case and finished his message, we read, "And with many other words he bore witness and continued to exhort them" (v. 40). When Peter finished his sermon that day, he pled for souls and pressed for decisions with the convicting power of the Holy Spirit. To put it in a crass, modern vernacular kind of way, he "asked for the sale." "With many other words," Peter pleaded with, exhorted, and encouraged the people to make a public commitment: an outward expression to accompany their inward decision to trust in the risen Christ. And the result? Three thousand happy new believers came out of the shadows to identify with Christ publicly and follow Him in believer's baptism.

It would be difficult to imagine a successful trial attorney not unashamedly asking the jury in his closing argument, with many other words, to make a decision in favor of his client. The attorney had spent weeks—more likely, months—preparing for the trial. He used his opening argument to present his case to the jury. He brought in witnesses to attest to the truth of his client's account. He precisely answered every objection raised. He introduced indisputable evidence and established facts into the case. He gave a well-thought-out, analytically convincing closing argument. Can you imagine this attorney after all that preparation, planning, and presenting then closing his briefcase and walking out of the courtroom without asking the jury to decide in favor of his client? And yet this happens too often with some of us, who have a much higher calling advocating for Christ and the gospel. We present our case and even call our witnesses, but then we close our Bibles and dismiss the people when the time comes to press for a decision.

The task of publicly calling people to repent and believe necessitates that a preacher ask himself a few questions. First, "*What?*" What does this passage specifically communicate about the gospel? And when I preach it, what can I do to ensure I convey its message about the gospel to my listeners? Second, ask yourself, "*So What?*" Will my message press unbelievers to repent and believe publicly and immediately? Finally, question yourself, "*Now What?*" In what specific ways can I clearly explain to unbelievers how they can repent of their sins and believe in Christ for salvation?

The volume you now hold in your hand is the first treatment of public gospel invitations that has emerged from a major publisher in thirty years. The first major treatise on this vital subject emerged in 1945 when Faris D. Whitesell, a professor at Northern Baptist Theological Seminary, published *65 Ways to Give Evangelistic Invitations*. In 1974 Roy Fish, the popular and longtime professor of evangelism at Southwestern Baptist Theological Seminary, wrote *Giving a Good Invitation*. It presented a biblical, theological, and historical defense, accompanied by helpful applications, for the offering of public gospel invitations. In 1984 R. Alan Streett, professor at Criswell College, published *The Effective Invitation: A Practical Guide for the Pastor*. During that same year, R. T. Kendall also published his passionate treatment of the public invitation in *Stand Up and Be Counted: Calling for Public Confession of Faith*. Finally, the last book on this subject, *Drawing the Net: 30 Practical Principles for Leading Others to Christ Publicly and Personally*, appeared in 1994 from the pen of the co-author of this volume, O. S. Hawkins. *The Gospel Invitation* will be especially helpful because it couples contributions from the academy with the practical experience of the pastorate into a single volume.

Denominations are dying. Some seminaries have removed evangelism classes from their curricula. Churches and networks are seeing commitments to Christ and baptisms plummet with every passing year. A growing number of evangelical pastors have discontinued the use of the public gospel invitation, opt-ing for a more nonconfrontational approach which results in little, if any, real exhortation or "pleading for souls" (a term we once used for the public invitation). Some do not publicly invite people to decide for Christ because they have never expe-rienced the effect of people coming forward; others have sincere theological reasons for not giving an invitation; some feel that not extending an invitation takes the pressure off the preach-ing experience; and still others have simply never been taught the "how-tos" of giving an effective, God honoring public invitation, void of manipulation. *The Gospel Invitation* is a call for reconsidering and rediscovering the effectiveness of asking people to make public their decision to follow Christ. The pages that follow will not only present the biblical, historical, and philosophical bases for public gospel invitations, but will also provide the busy pastor, preacher, or evangelist with practical and proven instructions to assist in the art of issuing Christ's own invitation to the lost.

One of the final verses in the Bible is an invitation for all posterity: "The Spirit and the Bride say, 'Come.' And let the one who hears say, 'Come'" (Rev 22:17). The Holy Spirit urges people to "come." He not only presses them to "come," but the Bride also invites people to "come." The Bride of Christ is composed of New Testament churches who are led by God-called pastors. Therefore, pastors are commissioned to extend an invitation for sinners to be saved whenever they preach.

Remember how the prophet Jonah initially refused to heed the call of God to invite the wicked people of Nineveh publicly to repent? When he came to his senses he declared, "Salvation belongs to the LORD!" (Jonah 2:9). In the mystery of God's ways, Scripture reveals that God stirs individual hearts and issues public invitations through those whom He sends.

As you, the reader, turn the page to begin this journey, we hope and pray that everyone who reads this book, especially those who are called to preach these unsearchable riches of Christ, will faithfully present the gospel message. When you finish your journey, we also pray that you will beseech others to respond to *The Gospel Invitation*!

O. S. HAWKINS, president emeritus, GuideStone
Financial Resources and former pastor of First
Baptist Church, Dallas, Texas

MATT QUEEN, professor and L. R. Scarborough
Chair of Evangelism ("Chair of Fire"), Southwestern
Baptist Theological Seminary, Fort Worth, Texas

PUBLIC INVITATIONS
IN THE BIBLE

ARE PUBLIC INVITATIONS BIBLICAL? GOSPEL PREACHERS OVER
the last few hundred years have exhorted people to repent and
believe by utilizing many different methods. Billy Sunday
popularized what we know now as altar calls during his tent
revivals when he implored his listeners to "hit the sawdust trail."
Counseling rooms in many of today's churches originated from
Charles Finney, who invited the unconverted to come and sit
on an "anxious bench" for prayer and spiritual counsel. Some
preachers and churches encourage those who want to receive
Christ to complete decision cards. Other churches possessing
technological expertise instruct attendees to text keywords or
scan QR codes to make their salvation decision known. These
churches then initiate a discipleship and follow-up process.

Because these various methods of exhortation cannot be
found in the Scriptures, some well-intending critics have dis-
couraged their use. However, the spirit and essence of public
invitations have been practiced in many different forms since
humans first sinned against God. Yes, public invitations are

indeed biblical! In fact, the Bible recounts numerous occasions in which God and His messengers publicly called people to obey Him immediately in the Old and New Testaments alike.

PUBLIC INVITATIONS IN THE OLD TESTAMENT

Public invitations in the Old Testament may look different from those in the New Testament. However, the intent of biblical invitations across both Testaments are the same—biblical invitations publicly call sinners to be reconciled to God. In the Old Testament God sometimes appeals to sinners on His own. At other times He makes appeals through His prophets. Nevertheless, Old Testament invitations set the pattern for extending public gospel invitations in both the New Testament and today. Consider a few examples from the Old Testament.

GOD'S CALL TO ADAM IN EDEN (GEN 3:6–21)

After creating everything, God commanded Adam and Eve not to eat fruit from the tree of the knowledge of good and evil. One day, while Adam and Eve were strolling through Eden, the sly serpent, Satan, enticed Eve to eat the forbidden fruit. Plucking the fresh produce from the tree, both she and Adam consumed it.

Instantaneously their sin was exposed. In an attempt to conceal their nakedness, Adam and Eve fashioned some leaves into makeshift clothing. They then heard the rustling of branches as the Lord God walked through the garden in the cool of the day. The leaves that concealed their nakedness could not cover up the overwhelming sense of guilt and shame Adam and Eve felt. They hid themselves behind some nearby trees, hoping they might obscure themselves and their sin from God's view.

Despite Adam's best attempts, he could not hide from the Lord's sight. Issuing the first public invitation in human history, the Lord Himself called out to Adam, "Where are you?" (3:9). God had no interest in initiating the world's first game of hide and seek. He already knew Adam's whereabouts and his wrongdoing. Instead, God publicly invited Adam to stop concealing what he had done in order to be confronted with his sin.

Adam immediately emerged from the canopy of trees covering him and initially confessed, "I heard the sound of you in the garden, and I was afraid, because I was naked, and I hid myself" (3:10). God asked Adam how he knew he was naked. In yet another attempt to conceal his complicity, Adam blamed Eve. She followed suit and indicted the serpent.

Each actor in this real-life scenario bore responsibility for disobeying the Divine. God judged and punished them for their unrighteousness. Adam would toil for the rest of his days with the ground that was now cursed on his behalf. Eve would experience pain in childbearing, and her desire would be for her husband. Because of Satan, all serpents would crawl on their bellies. And though Satan himself would bruise the heel of the woman's coming Offspring, her Seed would one day destroy him and his works under His feet.

Foreshadowing the atoning work of the Messiah, the Lord took the life of an innocent animal—the first death in the garden of life. When that little creature breathed its last breath, it was the first to know the expensive toll sin takes on a life. From its skin God made garments to supplant the leaves Adam and Eve had used to cover their nakedness.

In this first-ever public invitation, God extended a call to Adam and Eve. Once they publicly presented themselves before Him, He graciously clothed their nakedness with a covering of His own making.

MOSES'S DIRECTIVE WITHIN THE CAMP GATE
(EXOD 32:25–29)

A few thousand years later the Israelites, some of Adam's and Eve's descendants, found themselves in Egyptian captivity. God raised up Moses to become their leader and rescue them from Pharaoh's enslavement. Having escaped Pharaoh's forces by the Lord's intervention at the Red Sea, Israel traversed through the Wilderness of Sin to reach the Promised Land. Their wandering led them to the elevated peak—Mount Sinai. Smoke, thunder, and fire surrounded the mountain the day that God called down to Moses inviting him to come up and meet Him. The volcanic-looking mountain initially struck fear into the hearts of all Israel as they anxiously waited for Moses to return. Over time, however, their fear of the holy mount faded into familiarity.

"Moses is lost to us," they shouted to Aaron, Moses's brother. "Therefore, make other gods for us so we may worship them" (cf. Exod 32:1). Obliging their request, Aaron collected their golden earrings and melted them. He then fashioned a golden calf for them to worship, which closely resembled the Apis bull they had frequently seen their masters worship in Egypt. The next day Aaron even led them to celebrate this idolatrous deity, which he blasphemously called Yahweh (that is, the LORD), by singing, dancing, eating, and drinking before the idol.

Their idolatry incensed the Lord. Moses immediately interceded on the Israelites' behalf, and God consequently relented from destroying them. Moses returned to the camp with two tablets upon which God had inscribed His Law with His own finger. However, upon witnessing Israel's debauchery with his own eyes, Moses smashed the tablets and burned their golden god into ash.

Moses turned to his brother and indignantly asked, "How did they convince you to do this?" Aaron sheepishly replied,

"Moses, they thought you were dead and forced me to make gods for them. I took their gold from them, threw it all into the fire, and out came this calf" (cf. vv. 21–24). However, Moses knew better.

Although many of the people had scattered, Moses positioned himself within the gate of the camp so he could be seen and heard by those who remained. He publicly called his hearers to be reconciled to God with these words, "Who is on the LORD's side? Come to me" (v. 26). At that moment, the Levites moved toward him. In doing so, they openly aligned themselves with the Lord and with Moses, His servant. Everything about Moses's directive to the Levites and their public response thus qualifies it as one of the early public invitations in history.

JOSHUA'S CHOICE BEFORE THE TRIBES OF ISRAEL (JOSH 24:14–25)

Continuing the Mosaic tradition, the Lord told Joshua, "Moses my servant is dead. Now therefore arise, go over this Jordan, you and all this people, into the land that I am giving to them" (Josh 1:2). Three days later Joshua led Israel through the Jordan River upon dry land, just as Moses had done at the Red Sea. He led the tribes of Israel in war against the kings and people who occupied the Promised Land, and God gave His people victory over their enemies. Each tribe was apportioned its own territory, and the Promised Land had now become Israel's land.

Advanced in years, Joshua called for all of Israel and its leaders to present themselves before the Lord at Shechem. After they were assembled, he rehearsed everything the Lord had done for Israel through Abraham, Isaac, Jacob, and Moses, as well as himself. On the basis of God's faithfulness, Joshua publicly commanded them to fear the Lord, renounce the false gods of their past, and serve Him. He pressed them to consider what serving the Lord would mean: "And if it is evil in your eyes to serve the LORD, choose this day whom you will serve, whether the gods your fathers served in the region beyond the River, or the gods of the Amorites in whose land you dwell" (24:15a).

Before his hearers had the chance to respond, Joshua and his family publicly made their own choice. He declared, "But as for me and my house, we will serve the LORD" (v. 15b). All Israel then echoed, "We also will serve the LORD, for he is our God" (v. 18b). Doubting their resolve, Joshua responded by testing them: "You are not able to serve the LORD, for he is a holy God. He is a jealous God; he will not forgive your transgressions or your sins" (v. 19). They promptly replied, "No, but we will serve the LORD" (v. 21). Joshua recorded Israel's response in the Book of the Law as a public pledge of their decision. He memorialized it by positioning a large stone under an oak beside the sanctuary so they would never forget (v. 26).

ELIJAH'S CHALLENGE ON MOUNT CARMEL
(1 KGS 18:20–39)

Like Moses and Joshua before him, Elijah the Tishbite served as God's intermediary to call people to repentance. He declared a drought in Israel because of King Ahab's evil ways. In order to hide him from the king, God directed Elijah to sojourn at the brook Cherith. He was a prophet on the run. Later he stayed with a widow in Zarephath. And finally, after three years had passed, God sent Elijah to confront Ahab's profane idolatry that plagued all Israel.

"Are you finally showing yourself, O troubler of Israel?" Ahab inquired as Elijah approached him. "I am no trouble-maker, Ahab, but you and your priests are," the prophet retorted (cf. 1 Kgs 18:17–18). Elijah then provoked Ahab to assemble his and his wife's false prophets for a contest between their Canaanite gods, Baal and Asherah, and his God, Yahweh. The winner of this battle royal, Elijah suggested, would determine the true God in Israel.

Everyone in Israel gathered at Mount Carmel to witness this epic showdown between the false prophets and Elijah. Before the public competition could begin, an internal conflict ensued among the spectators. The so-called "Troubling Tishbite" took center stage and issued a public invitation to those in attendance: "How long are you going to struggle between two choices? If Yahweh is God, then follow Him, and if Baal is god, follow him." Unsure whom they would serve, they stood in silence (cf. v. 21). He pressed them further to decide:

> I, even I only, am left a prophet of the LORD, but Baal's prophets are 450 men. Let two bulls be given to us, and let them choose one bull for themselves and cut it in pieces and lay it on the wood, but put no fire to it. And I will prepare the other bull and lay it on the wood and put no fire to it. And you call upon the name of your god, and I will call upon the name of the LORD, and the God who answers by fire, he is God. (vv. 22–24a)

The terms of Elijah's proposal satisfied everyone. They all looked on with anticipation to see exactly whose God would answer with fire.

Baal's priests prepared their sacrifice, but no amount of their limping or leaping, calling or crying, and poking or prodding aroused Baal to produce fire. Elijah's point was taken—foreign gods are fake gods. Baal's prophets were embarrassed, but God's prophet was empowered! Elijah compelled Israel to come to him, and so they did. He then rebuilt Yahweh's altar which had fallen into ruin. Upon the altar he put wood, and on the wood he placed the bull, drenching them both with twelve large jars of water. Next, with a simple prayer Elijah asked God to show the people that He, indeed, was God and to turn their hearts back to Him. With mighty power the fire of the Lord then fell down from heaven, consuming the bull, the wood, the stones, the dust, and the water! The people responded to Elijah's "altar call," as it were, accompanied by God's mighty demonstration, by exclaiming, "The LORD, he is God; the LORD, he is God" (v. 39).

JOSIAH'S COMMAND TO JUDAH (2 CHR 34:29–33)

As the years passed, both Israel and Judah continued to vacillate between serving God and other gods. When they forsook God, which they did often, they aroused His anger and wrath against them. Around 628 BC King Josiah began to enact reforms to purge the wickedness in Judah that had provoked God. In the eighteenth year of Josiah's reign, Hilkiah the priest found the Book of the Law of Moses while repairing the house of the Lord. He gave it to Shaphan the scribe, who, in turn, brought it and read it to the king.

Josiah was overcome with grief and guilt when he heard the words of the Law, tearing his garments in repentance before God. He then sent for all of Judah—the elders, the priests, and all the inhabitants—to meet him at the house of the Lord in Jerusalem. When they arrived, he read the Book of the Law to them and made a public covenant with the Lord. Josiah then compelled those present to stand in solidarity with him in this covenant, and they assented. Roy Fish keenly observed that "Josiah did not seem to be afraid of 'putting too much pressure' on his people to get them to decide."[1]

ISAIAH'S REPORT STRENGTHENED BY THE LORD'S ARM (ISA 52:7–53:1)

While many Old Testament public invitations occur in narrative contexts, the prophetic books also preserve examples of public invitations. The prophecy of the Suffering Servant in

Isaiah 53 is quoted in the New Testament more than any other Old Testament passage. To be sure, Isaiah is not only prophesying about the coming Messiah, but he is preaching Jesus Christ—crucified, buried, and risen! However, have you ever noticed the invitation Isaiah references in this passage?

Isaiah begins this prophecy by writing, "Who has believed what he has heard from us? And to whom has the arm of the LORD been revealed?" (53:1). Whose report is Isaiah referencing? When did the Lord extend His arm? And why? The explanation is found a few verses earlier in chapter 52:

> How beautiful upon the mountains
>   are the feet of *him* who brings good news,
> who *publishes peace*, who *brings good news*
>   of happiness,
> who *publishes salvation*,
>   who says to Zion, "Your God reigns." . . .
> *The* LORD *has bared his holy arm*
>   before the eyes of all the nations,
> and all the ends of the earth shall see
>   the salvation of our God.
>   (vv. 7, 10, emphasis added)

The Jews were to respond by rejoicing in the good news of God's peace and salvation to Zion that the Lord's prophet, Isaiah, had brought and announced to them. The good news Isaiah published on the mountains sounds extremely similar to his description of the Suffering Servant in chapter 53. He proclaimed:

> Behold, my servant shall act wisely;
>   he shall be high and lifted up,
>   and shall be exalted.

As many were astonished at you—
   his appearance was so marred, beyond
   human semblance,
and his form beyond that of the children
   of mankind—
so shall he sprinkle many nations. (52:13–15a)

Furthermore, the Lord said He had displayed His holy arm
to the nations so they all might see His salvation. The "arm of
the LORD" is an idiom for the work and power of the Holy Spirit.
As Isaiah explained, "Kings shall shut their mouths because of
him, for that which has not been told them they see, and that
which they have not heard they understand" (v. 15b). So, kings
and rulers who neither have been told nor have ever heard about
God's Servant will recognize Him in His future rule and reign.
They will do so because the Lord's arm—the Holy Spirit—has
displayed God's salvation before all nations.

Isaiah's prophetic description of a gospel invitation (52:7, 10)
displays the cooperative nature of the divine and human dimensions in proclamation. This theme is continued in Isaiah 53 when
he prophesied and preached Jesus by inquiring, "Who has believed
the good news we have announced, and to whom has God's Spirit
revealed these things?" (cf. v. 1). Public invitations in the Bible
are not based solely on the preacher's extending them; they also
include the work of the Holy Spirit, who is empowering them.

Any preacher who extends public gospel invitations devoid
of the power of the Holy Spirit will likely practice some form of
manipulation, be it intentional or unintentional. Consequently,
such a preacher fails to meet the biblical aim and intent of preaching. In addition, any preacher who assumes that the work of the
Spirit in preaching frees him from any responsibility or obligation
to call men and women to repent and believe fails to emulate
biblical examples of preaching.

JONAH'S CRY THROUGHOUT NINEVEH (JONAH 3)

The overwhelming majority of Old Testament prophetic literature is concerned with God using His prophets to call Israel to repentance. However, God called Gentiles to repentance as well. For example, God commanded Jonah to go east to Nineveh in order to pronounce judgment on its inhabitants because of their wickedness. However, Jonah tried to evade God by traveling west to board a ship bound for Tarshish.

Jonah soon learned that no one can escape God's presence. God hurled a storm on the Mediterranean Sea that almost sank the vessel upon which he was sailing. The mariners then threw Jonah overboard to save the ship and themselves. The sinking prophet was tantalizing bait for a large, hungry fish. It swallowed him whole and ingested him for three days. Learning that no one can get away from God, Jonah prayed that God would save him. The Lord graciously heard his prayer and made the fish vomit Jonah onto dry land. At that point, Jonah heard God say a second time: "Go to Nineveh!" (cf. Jonah 3:2).

The reluctant prophet obeyed the Lord and traveled to Nineveh. Upon his arrival, he found the city to be much bigger than he expected. He could not just preach a drive-by sermon and return home; it was going to take him three days to deliver God's message to the Ninevites. Wasting no time, Jonah proclaimed: "Yet forty days, and Nineveh shall be overthrown!" (3:4)—a volatile punishment for a violent people. When the people heard that they only had forty days before God was going to visit Nineveh with judgment, they believed Him.

You may be asking yourself, "How could they believe in God? There's no invitation in the book of Jonah!" But there are indeed a few invitations in Jonah. First, Jonah's proclamation of God's judgment *is* a public invitation. As Josh Williams, Old Testament professor at Southwestern Seminary, has often said in his classroom, "The Old Testament prophets preached judgment through destruction in order to achieve repentance." This principle is found in Jeremiah 18:7–8, where the prophet wrote, "At one moment I might speak concerning a nation or concerning a kingdom to uproot, to pull down, or to destroy it; if that nation against which I have spoken turns from its evil, I will relent concerning the calamity I planned to bring on it" (NASB).

Second, the king of Nineveh, probably Ashur-dan III (773–755 BC), repented upon hearing Jonah and issued his own public proclamation to the entire city: "Let man and beast be covered with sackcloth, and let them call out mightily to God. Let everyone turn from his evil way and from the violence that is in his hands. Who knows? God may turn and relent and turn from his fierce anger, so that we may not perish" (Jonah 3:8–9). In response to the invitations offered by both Jonah and their king, the Ninevites publicly repented of their wickedness and God forgave them.

PUBLIC INVITATIONS IN THE NEW TESTAMENT

Invitations that called for public repentance in the Old Testament continued in the New Testament. From the Gospels to the Apocalypse, prophets, preachers, apostles, deacons, evangelists, and laity alike called people from every nation to repent of their sins and believe in Jesus Christ for salvation. Some appeals took place in personal or small group settings, but most were issued in the context of public preaching. Responses to these appeals varied. Many hearers immediately rejected the invitation, while some were open to hearing more in the future. However, others were persuaded, repented, believed, and were baptized. Consider the following examples.

JOHN THE BAPTIST'S MANY OTHER EXHORTATIONS (LUKE 3:7–18)

John the Baptist issued the first public invitation recorded in the New Testament. In it he preached a baptism of repentance for the forgiveness of sins. His public invitation to repent and be baptized caused his hearers to ponder, "What does it mean for us to repent?"

The crowd of common people in attendance were the first to verbalize their thoughts. "What then shall we do?" (Luke 3:10) they inquired of John. He responded, "Share your extra clothing and food with those who have none" (cf. v. 11). On the heels of John's answer, some tax collectors approached him and asked, "What about us?" He said to them, "Do not collect any more taxes from people than what you are required by law" (cf. vv. 12–13). Immediately some soldiers pushed their way through the crowd toward John. Many of the people probably thought they had come to arrest him. Instead, the soldiers also had a question for the prophet: "And we, what shall we do?" (v. 14a). John boldly told them, "Do not extort money from anyone by threats or by false accusation, and be content with your wages" (v. 14b).

Was the Baptizer preaching works salvation? No—he was preaching a salvation that works! Even after unbelievers hear a message and are convicted by the Holy Spirit to respond to it, they will not know how exactly to respond unless they are given specific instructions. Therefore, John described to the crowds, the tax collectors, and the soldiers what repentance would look like for each particular group if they were willing to be baptized in keeping with repentance—the crowds had to share their goods, the tax collectors had to forsake their greed, and the soldiers had to cease their bullying. In other words, the public preaching of the gospel will lead those who receive the gospel to practice it publicly.

John continued preaching the gospel by diverting the crowds' attention from himself to the soon-coming Messiah, Jesus Christ. He told them that when the Messiah would arrive, He would baptize them with the Holy Spirit and fire. Time was running out, however, for those who failed to repent, because He was also coming to judge.

John's message and mission were urgent. He continued to press the people to repent and be baptized: "So with many other exhortations he preached good news to the people" (v. 18). Luke uses similar wording when recounting Peter's Pentecost sermon (Acts 2:40), demonstrating that Peter and John issued the same type of public gospel invitation.

JESUS'S PREACHING THE GOSPEL OF GOD'S KINGDOM (MATT 4:17; MARK 1:14–15)

As previously observed, Isaiah 52:7–53:1 illustrated the human and divine dimensions of cooperation at work in publicly calling people to believe the good news. In their Gospels, Mark and Matthew included the ultimate representation of that divine-human collaboration by introducing the incarnate Christ—fully God and fully man—openly calling people to repentance. Matthew expressed this by writing, "From that time Jesus began to preach, saying, 'Repent, for the kingdom of heaven is at hand'" (Matt 4:17). In his own retelling of this incident, Mark recounted, "Jesus came . . . proclaiming the gospel of God, and saying, 'The time is fulfilled, and the kingdom of God is at hand; repent and believe in the gospel'" (Mark 1:14b–15).

When Matthew wrote, "Jesus began to preach, saying," the verbal tense he used indicated that whatever Jesus began preaching when He arrived in Capernaum continued to be proclaimed afterward. From this time and throughout His ministry, Jesus publicly and urgently called people to repent. The summary of this public invitation in Matthew 4:17, "Repent, for the kingdom of heaven is at hand," identically echoes John the Baptist's appeal in Matthew 3:2. Thus, both John's and Jesus's messages and public calls for decisions were indistinguishable.

Mark's account of this event adds a preceding phrase, "The time is fulfilled, and the kingdom of God is at hand," to Jesus's public call to repent and believe the good news. "The time is fulfilled" refers to the fulfillment of the Old Testament Scriptures. In other words, Jesus was informing His audience that the prophecies about the Messiah were being fulfilled at that moment. This same idea is in view when Paul centered the gospel upon Jesus's death, burial, and resurrection in 1 Corinthians 15:3–4. He explained that Christ's death and resurrection took place "in accordance with the Scriptures."

By adding, "the kingdom of God is at hand," Jesus declared Himself as the King over God's kingdom. As God's anointed King, He Himself would fulfill all of the Old Testament messianic prophecies. By calling for urgent and public repentance, Jesus surpasses being known, as many merely regard Him, as just a good teacher. His public appeal on this occasion, along with the many other exhortations that would follow in the Gospels, also identifies Him as a pleading preacher.

PETER'S MANY OTHER WORDS (ACTS 2:14–41)

Forty days after His resurrection, Jesus commanded His disciples "not to depart from Jerusalem, but to wait for the promise of the Father, which, he said, 'you heard from me; for John baptized with water, but you will be baptized with the Holy Spirit not many days from now'" (Acts 1:4b–5). Afterward Jesus ascended into heaven. Compliant with His instructions, His disciples waited for the Holy Spirit to arrive.

Because of Pentecost, Jewish pilgrims from around the world had come to Jerusalem to celebrate the festival. On this very day, the Holy Spirit filled the disciples and the place that they were staying. He manifested Himself in the disciples by causing them all to speak in various unfamiliar languages. The Jewish sojourners were both fascinated and intrigued by this strange phenomenon. All of them were able to understand in their own languages what the Spirit-filled disciples were saying. Some of them tried to figure out the meaning of this spectacle. Others mocked the disciples, thinking they were drunk.

Peter, the fisherman-turned-fisher-of-people, took his stand with the other apostles. He explained to the crowds that not only were the disciples sober, but they were speaking in the Spirit, just as Joel had foretold (Joel 2:28–32). He then preached Jesus to the people, demonstrating how He had fulfilled the messianic prophecies in the Psalms.

The Holy Spirit advanced beyond communicating through the mouths of the disciples and began convicting the hearts of the crowd. They desperately inquired, "Brothers, what shall we do?" (Acts 2:37). Peter then instructed them to repent and be baptized. As mentioned earlier, in the same way that John had preached with *many other exhortations* (Luke 3:18), Peter solemnly testified and *kept on exhorting* those in the crowd *with many other words* (Acts 2:40). In response to his extended pleas, those who received the gospel publicly pledged themselves to Christ's lordship through believer's baptism. Inasmuch, they were counted among the first members of the apostolic church in Jerusalem.

PETER'S AND JOHN'S ARRESTING APPEAL (ACTS 3:11–4:4)

A few days after Pentecost, Peter and John went to the temple around three o'clock in the afternoon. On their way inside to pray, they encountered a paralytic beggar at the gate called Beautiful. He caught their attention, and in turn they called for his attention. Peter then commanded him to walk in Jesus's name. Leaping from where he lay, the panhandler publicly praised God. The temple worshipers, who had intentionally looked the other way each day they had passed him, were now unable to take their eyes off him.

The man's healing encouraged the crowd to heed Peter and his words. Instead of making a name for himself, Peter made much about Jesus's name. He did so by preaching to them about His death and resurrection. In contrast to the man who had exhibited faith in His name, the crowd's rejection of Jesus as the Christ made them liable for His death. Peter implored them to repent of their unbelief and turn from their wicked ways. When they did this, the Lord would wipe away their sins, as well as refresh and bless them.

As much as the man's healing amazed the crowd, Peter's preaching of Jesus and His resurrection agitated the Sadducees, who did not believe in a resurrection. They, along with the temple guard, abruptly interrupted Peter's public call for the people's repentance, and they arrested him and John. However, the penalty that awaited the crowd for believing in the resurrected Christ paled in comparison to the penalty they realized Jesus had paid for them on the cross. Right then and there, around five thousand of them publicly responded to Peter's message, placing their faith in Jesus Christ.

PAUL'S ADDRESS TO THE PHILOSOPHERS (ACTS 17:16–34)

Arriving in Athens alone, Paul made his way to the synagogue, as was his custom. He reasoned with the Jews that Jesus was the Christ. In the city marketplace, he also proclaimed Jesus and His resurrection. Some Epicurean and Stoic philosophers were among those in the marketplace. They heard him preaching Jesus and the resurrection. Supposing he was introducing the Athenians to a new deity, Jesus, and His female consort,

Anastasia (the Greek word for *resurrection*), they invited him atop the Areopagus so they could learn more about these new gods.

Seeking to correct the Athenians' misunderstanding of what he had preached, Paul referenced an altar to an unknown god among the pantheon of deities they worshiped. He contrasted that god, whom they did not know, with the God that he both knew and preached. His God, Paul explained, created everything in the world, determined how all the peoples of the world would live, and sent His righteous Son to die and be raised from the dead. In order that people may escape the impending judgment that God will bring upon the world, He has commanded everyone, everywhere to repent.

Upon hearing that Paul was talking about the resurrection of the dead, not a female deity named Anastasia, everyone openly responded in one of three ways. Several of them mocked Paul; some were curious and desired to talk with him again about Jesus and the resurrection; and a few of them even believed, joining Paul.

PAUL'S ALMOST PERSUADING AGRIPPA TO BECOME A CHRISTIAN (ACTS 26:27–29)

Having appealed to Caesar in response to charges of inciting civil unrest brought against him by Jews in Jerusalem, Paul was first summoned to appear before King Agrippa. Agrippa and his sister Bernice, both client rulers of the Herodian dynasty in Judea, entered the auditorium in Caesarea with great pomp and circumstance, accompanied by Roman military commanders and the prominent men of the city.

Agrippa invited Paul to answer the accusations against him. He obliged the king, and went on to share his testimony of faith in Jesus Christ. After Paul appealed to the Scriptures while preaching Christ's death and resurrection, the Roman governor Porcius Festus interrupted him, "Paul, you are out of your mind;

your great learning is driving you out of your mind" (v. 24b). Undeterred, Paul turned to Agrippa and asked in the presence of all the court, "King Agrippa, do you believe the prophets? I know that you believe" (v. 27).

The king, somewhat taken aback by the urgency of Paul's question, replied with his own query, "Are you trying to persuade me to become a Christian in such a short amount of time, Paul?" (cf. v. 28). Giving him one more chance to respond, Paul pleaded, "Whether [in a] short or long [time], I would to God that not only you but also all who hear me this day might become such as I am—except for these chains" (v. 29). However, the king was unmoved. As far as anyone knows, neither he nor anyone in his court pledged themselves to the lordship of Christ.

CONCLUSION

While the forms of public invitations in the Bible vary, they all express a uniform intent: to call sinners to be publicly reconciled to God. This chapter's survey of public invitations in the Old and New Testaments yields four important conclusions that should inform contemporary gospel invitations. Implementing them will assist everyone who issues gospel appeals today.

First, gospel preachers must precisely and clearly call for decisions with a sense of immediacy. In the Old Testament Moses, Joshua, and Elijah confidently stood as spokesmen for the God of Israel before those who worshiped other gods. These prophetic men boldly confronted their hearers with a clear choice to make: continue to serve their false gods, or turn away from their idols and align themselves with the one true God—Yahweh. With no knowledge about how many of those listening, if any, would join them, these leaders visibly declared that they had chosen the Lord's side. They candidly challenged their audience to choose, at that very moment, the one true God or the gods whom they had been serving.

In like manner, preachers in the New Testament pointedly called for instantaneous decisions. John the Baptist, Jesus, Peter, and Paul alike urged both Jews and Gentiles to repent immediately. Unbelievers were encouraged to respond right away to both the message they heard and the Holy Spirit's conviction of their sins. Several, such as those who heard John on the banks of the Jordan and the Jewish pilgrims who listened to Peter at Pentecost, repented and believed on the spot. Others, like the indecisive philosophers on the Areopagus, pledged to hear Paul again on the matter; however, the Bible never records an occasion in which they did. And some, like Agrippa, recognized the preacher's plea for an immediate decision and instead chose to walk away.

Therefore, in order to follow these examples found in the Scriptures, gospel invitations must incorporate both the *how* and the *now*. In doing so, preachers should precisely explain *how* those convicted by the Spirit should repent of their sins and believe in Christ for salvation. They should also urge their hearers not to delay but to respond and act *now*.

Second, those who proclaim the good news must be motivated by God's compassion for the wicked. Love served as a primary motivation for almost every person in the Scriptures who issued a public invitation. For example, even though Adam had sinned against Him in the garden, God compassionately called out to Adam rather than destroying him. Furthermore, He declared that the woman's Seed—the Messiah—would victoriously crush the serpent's head, and He took the life of an animal to cover Adam and his wife's nakedness. God's inquiring call, His pronouncement of conquest, and the animal-skin clothing He made for the first transgressors were all borne out of His deep and abiding love for humankind.

Moses cared for the Israelites when he asked them, "Who is on the LORD's side?" (cf. Exod 32:26). Moses's love for his people was so profound that he climbed Mount Sinai the day after the incident of the golden calf and pled with the Lord to forgive them. He said to God, "Alas, this people has sinned a great sin. They have made for themselves gods of gold. But now, if you will forgive their sin—but if not, please blot me out of your book that you have written" (vv. 31b–32). In other words, if God would not forgive the Israelites, Moses's love for them led him to pledge that he was willing to lose his life either in the here or in the hereafter.

God's messengers in the New Testament also expressed love for the people whom they publicly invited to repent and believe. For instance, before Jesus commanded the rich young ruler, "Go, sell all that you have and give to the poor, and you will have treasure in heaven; and come, follow me" (Mark 10:21b), Luke described that "Jesus, looking at him, *loved* him" (v. 21a, emphasis added). Also, consider how Jesus (Matt 23:37–39) and Paul (Rom 9:1–3; 10:1) desired that their kinsmen would respond to the gospel by believing in the Messiah. Furthermore, Paul told the Corinthians that his persuasion and appeal for unbelievers to be reconciled to God was controlled by the love of Christ (2 Cor 5:14).

Only Jonah went to Nineveh without loving those to whom he would preach. Although he professed orthodoxy (cf. Jonah 1:9) and practiced orthopraxy (cf. 3:3a), he still lacked a right concern toward those to whom he told God's message. Jonah failed to adopt God's love and concern for the Ninevites.

After Jonah pronounced God's judgment upon them, the inhabitants of Nineveh repented, and God responded by relenting from the disaster He was going to bring upon them. Both of these incidents angered Jonah. He prayed to God, "O LORD, is not this what I said when I was yet in my country? That is why I made haste to flee to Tarshish; for I knew that you are a gracious God and merciful, slow to anger and abounding in steadfast love, and relenting from disaster. Therefore now, O LORD, please take my life from me, for it is better for me to die than to live" (4:2b–3). Jonah's confession revealed why he initially ran from God's call—God was compassionate and loving, desiring that the wicked not be destroyed.

Jonah failed to love the sinful Ninevites because he was full of loving himself. He went to the east side of the city to witness if God would do anything to Nineveh. The Lord created a plant to provide Jonah shade and then sent a worm to destroy it. Exposed to the sun and the east wind, Jonah became so miserable that he wanted to die. God then confronted him about his attitude toward those to whom he had preached, saying, "You pity the plant, for which you did not labor, nor did you make it grow, which came into being in a night and perished in a night. And should not I pity Nineveh, that great city, in which there are more than 120,000 persons who do not know their right hand from their left, and also much cattle?" (vv. 10–11).

Therefore, preachers of the gospel must issue their invitations to repent and believe with a sincere sense of love for unbelievers. While God can and has saved people whether or not the one sharing with them truly cared for them, He still wants His heralds to love sinners because He loves them. Ministers who lack a love for the lost will also find their hearts and even their preaching grow cold and insensitive. Therefore, in order to love those far from God, preachers should intentionally pray for the salvation of unbelievers whom they personally know, as well as for those whom they may not know but who will sit under their preaching on any given Sunday.

Third, gospel preachers must seek the help of the Holy Spirit to convict and convince their hearers when they extend public invitations. Both the Old and New Testaments necessitate that human agents work in conjunction with and dependent upon the power of divine agency in calling for faith decisions. For example, Isaiah introduced his prophecy of the Suffering Servant by linking his preaching with the work of the Holy Spirit (cf. Isa 53:1). John made this same connection in concluding Revelation by writing, "The *Spirit* and the *Bride* say, 'Come.' And let the one who hears say, 'Come.' And let the one who is thirsty come; let the one who desires take the water of life without price" (Rev 22:17, emphasis added). As such, the Holy Spirit and the Bride of Christ delivered the final invitation in the Bible in unison.

At Pentecost the Holy Spirit filled the disciples of Jesus (Acts 2:1–12) so that every pilgrim visiting Jerusalem that day could hear them in their own language. The Spirit then worked in concert with Peter's evangelistic sermon to "cut" the hearers' hearts (v. 37). His conviction prompted them to ask Peter what they should do. The apostle then commanded them to repent and be baptized. As a result, three thousand responded to his appeal and were baptized.

Any preacher who does not depend upon God the Spirit when he preaches has failed before he has begun. No preacher, no matter how experienced, winsome, prepared, or gifted he is, has the ability to persuade unbelievers to repent and believe in his own power. He requires the help of the Spirit to fill him and work in the hearts of those who hear him preach.

When the Spirit convicts people who hear the good news, those who share it are not interfering with His work by explaining how inquirers can receive God's forgiveness. Lost people do not know how to respond to the gospel, even after they have heard it and have been convicted by it. Therefore, preachers must advise unbelievers with specific instructions of how to repent and believe in order that they may receive Christ. Doing so imitates the faithful examples of men like John the Baptist (Luke 3:10–14), Peter (Acts 2:37–41), and Paul (16:30–33).

Finally, ministers of the gospel must not consider their gospel invitations a failure if no one or only a few respond. A preacher will not witness someone coming to Christ every time he shares the gospel and calls for a response. But he will never see someone come to Christ if he never issues an invitation to do so. In fact, almost, if not every, prophet and preacher in the Bible had more people reject their appeals than received them.

Consider Jeremiah's ministry and the number of people that responded to it—not many at all. Also recall in Isaiah 6, when the prophet declared, "Here I am! Send me" (v. 8b), that God then told him that the people would not understand or perceive what he would tell them. The New Testament is also replete with occasions in the ministries of John the Baptist, Jesus, Peter, Stephen, and Paul when their evangelistic summons were rejected. However, neither they nor their appeals were failures.

In fact, those in the New Testament who preached for a verdict deemed what they did a "success" despite any negative results. For example, when Peter and John were released from being detained and punished for preaching the gospel at Solomon's Portico, they found more fulfillment in the fidelity of their preaching (Acts 5:41) than they did in the fruit of their preaching (v. 14). Even Paul articulated a similar sentiment in his farewell to the Ephesian elders, beginning his address by righteously boasting that the rejection he faced from the Jews did not demur him from boldly preaching "repentance toward God and of faith in our Lord Jesus Christ" (Acts 20:18–21).

Every time a preacher communicates the gospel and offers an invitation to receive it he is successful, regardless of how those who hear it respond, for at least three reasons. First, God, not the preacher, is responsible any time unbelievers respond in repentance and faith to the preached Word. Consequently, heralds of the good news cannot take credit for the salvation of anyone who receives the message they preach. Second, sinners who do not accept the gospel that is extended to them do so because of their own disobedience to the Spirit and the Word. In such cases they, not the ministers who invited them to repent and believe, bear responsibility for not accepting Christ. Finally, inviting people to trust in Christ fulfills New Testament commands to exhort unbelievers to believe the truth. Therefore, invitations should be considered successful because they are an expression of a gospel preacher's obedience to both the Lord and His Word.

THE NECESSITY OF PUBLIC GOSPEL INVITATIONS

THE PUBLIC GOSPEL INVITATION HAS BEEN CRITICIZED BY preachers on opposing sides of the philosophical and theological spectrums. Some well-meaning discipleship experts are convinced that disciples can be made only over a prolonged period of time in a relationship context, while a few soteriological determinists accuse those who use invitations of engaging either in manipulation or interference with the Spirit's work. A growing number of ministry pragmatists also claim, "Invitations no longer work." Although a growing number of pastors and preachers have abandoned the use of public invitations in their sermons, the need to call men, women, boys, and girls publicly to profess their faith in Jesus Christ has never been more urgent.

WHY GOSPEL INVITATIONS ARE NECESSARY

The biblical examples from the previous chapter serve as justification for preachers to offer gospel invitations in the context of public preaching. What other reasons support the use of invitations today? Gospel invitations should be offered in public settings because of: (1) the New Testament's precedent of publicly issuing gospel invitations in order to make disciples; (2) unbelievers' lack of familiarity in knowing how to respond to gospel invitations when they are convicted of their sins by the Spirit; (3) the implicit nature of preaching and its relationship to gospel invitations; and (4) the historical record of how preachers have issued gospel invitations that God has used to bring people to faith in Christ.

THE NEW TESTAMENT PRECEDENT OF MAKING DISCIPLES INSTANTANEOUSLY THROUGH PREACHING

The Gospels describe Jesus's ministry primarily as one of instantaneous disciple-making through preaching. This observation, however, does not mean that He neglected the practice of personal disciple-making. Two early incidents of Jesus's public calling of disciples occurred when He appealed that (1) the crowds should repent and believe the gospel (Matt 4:17; Mark 1:14–15) and (2) select Galilean fishermen should follow Him and become fishers of people (Matt 4:19; Mark 1:17; cf. Luke 5:10). The context of these occasions indicate that Jesus's hearers responded publicly and immediately to His call. Furthermore, early in his Gospel, John describes the ministerial activity of Jesus and His followers as "making and baptizing . . . disciples" (John 4:1–2; cf. 3:22). The large numbers of disciples that Jesus made and who His few followers, in turn, baptized implies these occurred as a result of public preaching, not one-on-one conversations (although Jesus practiced conversational disciple-making throughout the Fourth Gospel, e.g., 1:40–51; 3:1–10; 4:7–26; [7:53–8:11]; 9:35–41).

Not only did Jesus make disciples through His own preaching, but He commissioned His disciples to do likewise. Matthew

10, Mark 6, and Luke 9 and 10 all recount Jesus's sending followers to preach with the intent that those who would hear their message would also immediately respond—positively or negatively.

Jesus anticipated that not everyone would repent and believe the disciples' message. For this reason, He instructed His followers to shake the dust off their feet whenever anyone would reject their message upon hearing it (Matt 10:14; Mark 6:11; Luke 9:5). Shaking the dust off one's feet or garments was a gesture pronouncing indictment against a preacher's hearers for rejecting his message about the kingdom of God. The New Testament documents only two occurrences of this practice, and in both cases it took place in the context of Paul's making disciples through preaching. In Acts 13:51, Paul and Barnabas "shook off the dust from their feet against" the Jews who had incited and instigated persecution against them for boldly speaking the gospel. And in Acts 18:6, Paul shook out his garments, resembling Nehemiah's dramatic warning to those Jewish nobles and officials who were unjustly exacting interest from their countrymen (Neh 5:13). By emulating Nehemiah in this manner, Paul indicted the Jews in the synagogue who had rejected his preaching of Jesus as the Messiah.

Before He ascended back into heaven, Jesus commanded His disciples, "Go therefore and *make disciples* of all nations, baptizing them in the name of the Father and of the Son and of the Holy Spirit, teaching them to observe all that I have commanded you" (Matt 28:19–20a, emphasis added). These disciples, eleven of whom would serve as His apostles, went to Jerusalem to wait for the Holy Spirit. Upon receiving the Spirit, they publicly began supernaturally speaking in the tongues of the Jewish pilgrims from all over the then-known world. Peter stood with the rest of the apostles and preached from Joel and the Psalms. As a result of the Spirit's work in, through, and around them, Peter and the disciples made three thousand new disciples, whom they immediately baptized and then taught obedience to Christ's commands (Acts 2:41–47).

Not every public attempt to make disciples in Acts was met with such a reception. Stephen, the first Christian martyr, preached with the intent that his listeners, being convicted by the Spirit (cf. 7:51, 54), would immediately and publicly turn and follow Christ. Unlike the response that Peter received, Stephen's audience rigidly rejected his word. In fact, Stephen indicated by crying out, "Lord, do not hold this sin against them" (v. 60) that their instant rejection of him, his message about Christ, and the Spirit's conviction constituted sin.

Other early disciples also put into practice Jesus's command to make disciples. For example, Luke recorded that Philip was making disciples and baptizing them (8:4–40). He also highlighted some men from Cyprus and Cyrene who preached Christ and witnessed multitudes turning to the Lord (11:20–26), and extensively covered the ministry of Paul (13:14–52; 14:1, 20–21; 16:12–15, 25–34; 17:1–4, 10–12, 16–34; 18:4–8; 19:1–7, 21–26; 28:16–24). Each of these occasions occurred when the disciples preached the gospel in public settings. In fact, the predominate method by which most Christian disciples were both made and baptized in the New Testament took place when preachers issued public appeals for their hearers to repent and believe immediately.

The majority of these disciple-making instances in Acts are attributed to Paul. Luke described them as persuasion (17:4; 18:4; 19:26; 26:27–29; 28:23; cf. 2 Cor 5:11, which evidences Paul's corroboration). Paul's method and practice of persuasion, however, was not conducted through manipulative means. Instead, it was empowered by and in concert with the convincing and convicting work of the Holy Spirit.

The public precedent to make disciples still applies to

preachers today. Although disciple-making methods vary from Christian to Christian, preaching is the primary way that every pastor should attempt to make disciples. As this section demonstrates, examples and precedents for making disciples are replete throughout the Gospels and Acts. In order to make disciples through public proclamation, those who preach must urgently appeal for hearers to repent and believe. Otherwise, how else will unbelievers who are convicted by the Holy Spirit upon hearing the Word know how to respond in order to become baptized, obedient disciples? Making disciples through preaching does not mean, as some may suppose, that those who do so compete with God in receiving the credit for any results. Instead, publicly making disciples means the preachers' actions are in complete compliance with God's authoritative directive to make, by the power of His Holy Spirit, disciples of all peoples.

THE INCOMPREHENSION OF UNBELIEVERS TO RESPOND TO THE GOSPEL

The Bible teaches that unbelieving men and women possess neither the ability to save themselves nor any desire to be saved from their sins. Also, apart from a witness of the gospel, they neither know about salvation through Christ nor know how they can become recipients of it through repentance and faith. Evangelism and conversion narratives in the New Testament corroborate these axioms, while also teaching that God does not save unbelievers apart from (1) their hearing the gospel (cf. Rom 10:17) and (2) the Holy Spirit convicting them of their sin and convincing them to repent and believe in Christ (cf. John 16:8–11; Acts 2:37). In fact, even after hearing the good news and being convicted, some unbelievers still do not specifically know how to become a Christian unless a human agent provides instructions to them. How do these principles inform and relate to the issuing of gospel invitations in public settings?

The New Testament presents at least three occasions when unbelievers heard about the good news in some public forum and were prompted by the Holy Spirit to respond to it, yet did not know what to do. When these situations occurred, how should the preacher of the gospel have proceeded? Should he have told those asking for instruction about what they should do that any exhortation beyond the message he preached would infringe upon the Holy Spirit's work? Would any additional instruction he had offered be manipulation? Was it biblically permissible for him to counsel those moved by both the Word and the Spirit to repent and believe immediately?

The first of these incidents occurred in Luke 3:2b–18, when John the Baptist was preaching a baptism of repentance for the forgiveness of sins in the region around the Jordan River. Luke described John's message as "good news" (v. 18). Crowds of people came for him to baptize them, and he publicly urged them, "You brood of vipers! Who warned you to flee from the wrath to come? Bear fruits in keeping with repentance" (vv. 7b–8a). Three distinct groups of people—the crowds, the tax collectors, and the soldiers—all then asked him, "What are we supposed to do?" (cf. v. 10).

These people had publicly heard John proclaim the good news of forgiveness and call them to repentance. Their desire to undergo a baptism of repentance, as well as their inquiry about how to bear fruit, indicated that they were being convicted by the Spirit to respond to the gospel. Otherwise, how could they, as depraved human agents, act in this manner? Nevertheless, these groups of people were completely perplexed about what they were being implored to do.

John showed no hesitation to instruct the groups publicly in ways that they could demonstrate evidence of their genuine repentance. Furthermore, he neither viewed doing so as violating the work of the Spirit in salvation, nor did he seem to consider his strong language (e.g., "You brood of vipers!") in exhorting them as a manipulative way to shame them into a decision. Instead, John continued admonishing the crowds by instructing them, "Whoever has two tunics is to share with him who has none, and whoever has food is to do likewise" (v. 11). He advised the tax collectors, "Collect no more than you are authorized to do" (v. 13). He counseled the soldiers, "Do not extort money from anyone by threats or by false accusation, and be content with your wages" (v. 14). By publicly preaching the gospel, boldly calling for his hearers to receive his message, and specifically explaining to them how they were to respond to it, John helped them comprehend what the Word and the Spirit required of them.

A second example took place in Acts 2:14–41, when Peter preached Christ during Pentecost to pilgrims of the Diaspora who had gathered in Jerusalem to observe the Feast. Upon hearing Jesus's disciples speak in tongues as the Spirit gave them ability, these Jewish worshipers were perplexed and amazed.

In response, Peter explained that the phenomena they were witnessing was a fulfillment of Joel 2:28–32. He then preached Jesus's life, death, burial, and resurrection to them from Psalm 16:8–11 and 110:1. Upon Peter's declaration that they should "know for certain that God has made [this Jesus] both Lord and Christ" (Acts 2:36), the Holy Spirit convicted them of their guilt by piercing them to the heart. They desperately questioned, "Brothers, what shall we do?" (v. 37).

Peter did not respond, "I am unable to tell you what to do, because if I did I would be interfering with what the Holy Spirit is doing in your heart."[1] Neither did he exploitatively capitalize on the crowd's bewilderment concerning the supernatural phenomena they witnessed. Instead, Peter commanded them to make a public pledge to follow Christ in cooperation with what the Spirit was doing in them and through him. He said, "Repent and be baptized every one of you in the name of Jesus Christ for the forgiveness of your sins, and you will receive the gift of the Holy Spirit. . . . Save yourselves from this crooked generation" (vv. 38, 40b). Peter's instruction to clarify the crowd's curiosity about the message they heard and the conviction they experienced led them to become baptized, obedient disciples publicly and immediately (vv. 41–46).

Finally, a similar occurrence took place in Acts 16:11–34 among a smaller group of people than the previous two episodes—prisoners in a jail and the jailer's family. By way of divine direction, Paul, Silas, and their missionary companions had found themselves in the Roman colony of Philippi. They encountered and evangelized a prominent woman of the city, Lydia, who believed and was baptized upon hearing the gospel.

On another day, the missionaries were traveling to the riverside place of prayer. Following them was a demon-possessed fortune teller shouting, "These men are servants of the Most High God, who proclaim to you the way of salvation" (v. 17). Paul cast the demon out of her, rendering her unable to earn any more fortune-telling money for her masters. They angrily dragged Paul and Silas before the magistrates of the town and incited the crowd against them. After being stripped and beaten, Paul and Silas were ordered to be detained in the city's prison.

Luke recounted that Paul and Silas prayed and sang hymns to God in the prison while the other inmates listened to them. Suddenly an earthquake shook the prison's foundation, opened the doors, and loosed the prisoners' bonds. The jailer, assuming that his prisoners had escaped and that he would be executed by the magistrates, drew his sword to commit suicide. However, Paul stopped him and informed him that no one had fled. The jailer fearfully fell down before Paul and Silas and asked, "Sirs, what must I do to be saved?" (v. 30).

Was the jailer asking how his physical life could be spared, or was he inquiring how he could be saved from his sins through Jesus? New Testament scholar John Polhill addressed this question by stating:

> It has often been argued that his question ("What must I do to be saved?") was intended in the secular sense of the word "salvation," that he was asking how his life should be spared. But his life had already been spared. No one had escaped. More likely he asked about his salvation in the full religious sense. Perhaps he had heard the servant girl's proclamation that Paul spoke of the way of salvation (v. 17). Perhaps he had heard Paul's preaching or reports of his preaching but had not fully understood. Perhaps he had fallen asleep to the sound of Paul and Silas's hymns to God. Now he was ready for understanding. The miracle of the earthquake and the prisoners who wouldn't flee arrested his attention and prepared his heart to receive Paul's message.[2]

As the person responsible for the jail, he knew the reasons why each inmate, including Paul and Silas, had been detained. Their trouble in Philippi had begun because they had been proclaiming about "the way of salvation" (v. 17).

Even though Luke did not record that Paul was preaching while he and Silas prayed and sang, he could have been doing so. References to Paul's imprisonment in Acts, as well as in his epistles, indicate that he regularly preached the gospel while being held in custody. So, although it cannot be proven, it is likely that he also preached during his incarceration in Philippi. Even if Paul did not preach the gospel in the traditional sense, it was likely preached through the two men's prayers and singing. Perhaps one of the hymns they sang was a primitive form of the one Paul wrote in Philippians 2:5–11.

However, the most convincing evidence that the intent of the jailer's question dealt with the salvation of his soul comes from Paul's reply: "Believe in the Lord Jesus, and you will be saved, you and your household" (Acts 16:31). Instead of informing Paul and Silas that they had misunderstood his query, the jailer and his family listened to the words they brought from the Lord. Paul did not use the supernaturally timed earthquake that opened the jail nor the jailer's fear of death to pressure him into belief. In the end, the jailer and his household, and perhaps other prisoners as well, were baptized upon their hearing of the gospel.

As these three episodes of public gospel preaching attest, the depravity of sin prevents unbelievers from knowing what to do with the gospel, even after they hear someone preach it and feel the Spirit's conviction about it. For this reason, preachers should issue public gospel invitations with specific instructions about how to repent and believe. These invitations can, and should, be practiced in a way that neither violates the work of the Holy Spirit in salvation nor attempts to manipulate sinners into insincere decisions.

THE IMPLICIT NATURE OF PREACHING AND ITS DISTINCTION FROM TEACHING

The implicit nature of Christian preaching necessitates that preachers appeal for their hearers to commit to the message. Christian teaching, on the other hand, intends to convey and impart truth and information to learners. Jonathan T. Pennington has offered an extremely helpful way to distinguish preaching from teaching in the Christian context. He wrote:

> We can define preaching as *the invitational and exhortational proclamation of biblical and theological truth*. Teaching, by contrast, is *the explanation and explication of biblical and theological truth*.

> What is shared between Christian preaching and teaching
> is the content—biblical and theological truth. The difference
> lies in the mode and immediate goal.[3]

Nevertheless, many people who publicly proclaim the Word commonly confuse or conflate the differentiating marks between these two noble activities.

The distinction between preaching and teaching can be traced back to the inception of primitive Christianity itself. In his seminal volume, *The Apostolic Preaching and Its Developments*, C. H. Dodd investigated the content of the message first-century Christians preached about Jesus. He quickly learned that the New Testament contained two kinds of content—doctrine and gospel. Both types of instruction were shaped by the form in which the apostles, writers, or preachers communicated them— that is, through teaching (doctrine) and preaching (gospel). He wrote:

> The New Testament writers draw a clear distinction between preaching and teaching. Teaching . . . is in a large majority of cases ethical instruction[,] . . . apologetic, [and] sometimes . . . it includes the exposition of theological doctrine. Preaching, on the other hand, is the public proclamation of Christianity to the non-Christian world.[4]

Although he drew some erroneous conclusions about the differences between preaching and teaching as they relate to the nature of evangelism and discipleship, Dodd's introduction of these distinctions became a standard way for Protestants to conceptualize the two activities.

Building on Dodd's work, Michael Green extended the common understanding of public gospel proclamation in the New Testament. He explained that first-century Christian preaching, as opposed to teaching, *"looked for a response.* The apostles were not shy about asking people to decide for or against the God who had decided for them. They expected results. They challenged people to do something about the message they had heard."[5] Green claimed that the appeal and anticipation for a response in preaching was characteristic of all preaching at that time. Roy Fish agreed with Green's sentiment, asserting, "One distinction of New Testament preaching was the preacher and invitation were virtually inseparable. The very nature of the message they preached compelled them to appeal for response."[6]

Preachers need to retain the biblical distinction between the aims and forms of Christian preaching and teaching. If they do, when they preach they ought to call for and expect a response on the part of their hearers. "Good preaching pleads with people to respond to the Word of God," explained John Piper.[7] Therefore, as L. R. Scarborough has posited, "All preaching, whether didactic, apologetic, hortatory, expository or soul-saving, should be in the evangelistic spirit."[8] Preaching that is considered evangelistic must undoubtedly engage in the task of exhortation.

The *New International Dictionary of New Testament Theology* explains *exhortation* this way: "Teaching has primarily to do with imparting intellectual insight and knowledge, and education . . . [and] is often thought to be limited to a person's formative years. But to exhort means to exert influence upon the will and the decision of another with the object of guiding him to observe certain instructions."[9] Additionally, J. Josh Smith has argued that those who preach must be committed to the biblical imperative to exhort those who hear their preaching. He wrote:

> The scriptural admonitions and examples for preaching indicate that the preacher does, in fact, have a responsibility to call people to obedience. . . . Preaching is calling for a verdict.

Preaching for a verdict is preaching that exhorts. The call to exhort is the call to speak to the will of the hearer, not just to inform the mind of the hearer. It is pleading, persuading, and strongly urging the hearer to respond in obedience to the Word of God. It moves beyond suggested application into a definitive call to respond. While application might explain what the text demands, exhortation pleads with the hearer to respond to its demands. Exhortation speaks directly to the will.[10]

Exhortation and persuasion, words that the authors of the New Testament paired with the act of preaching, are necessary in order for someone to proclaim the Word publicly. However, practicing one or both does not necessarily constitute manipulation, nor should they be used as a license to do so.

In conclusion, the nature and purpose of biblical preaching can be distinguished from the nature and purpose of biblical teaching. Expositional, as well as text-driven, preaching principally aims to convince both believing and unbelieving hearers to change in conformity to the text of Scripture, whereas biblical teaching primarily seeks to instruct hearers with the truth of the text so that they may gain understanding of it. Because this distinction exists, and since exhortation serves as the differentiating mark of preaching, those who publicly proclaim the Word should employ gospel invitations.

THE HISTORIC USE OF PUBLIC GOSPEL INVITATIONS

Most criticisms against public invitations have followed along methodological lines. Specifically, both the system and techniques of so-called "altar calls" have been critiqued. However, as observed in the previous chapter, public invitations took various forms and were employed differently throughout the Scriptures. While some templates of how to issue gospel invitations will be suggested in later chapters, this book's aim is not to argue *how* preachers must extend an invitation to respond to God's Spirit and the proclamation of His Word. Rather, it argues *that* they must issue invitations to repent and believe to those under their hearing.

While manipulative and aberrative public invitations have been thoroughly documented throughout history, an innumerable number of genuine conversions have also resulted from the use of public invitations. R. Alan Streett most notably sustained this claim in *The Effective Invitation: A Practical Guide for the Pastor* when he demonstrated and documented historical examples of people who received Christ as a result of public gospel invitations.[11] In fact, more people have likely been converted by responding to public invitations associated with preaching than by any other evangelistic means.

How prominent, if at all, were public invitations to receive Christ throughout church history? While Charles Finney is universally associated with popularizing what is commonly referred to as the "altar call" and "establishing it in the evangelical mind [until today] as the essential accompaniment [to] . . . preaching," should he also be credited as the one responsible for urging immediate and public decisions through preaching?[12] Were such appeals an invention or innovation of the nineteenth century, or can they be traced back to the first century? Indeed, a cursory review of the spread of the gospel throughout history yields a consistent practice of publicly and immediately calling people to repent and believe in Jesus Christ for salvation in many different forms and by various means.

The previous chapter provided evidence that apostolic preaching in the New Testament included the use of public invitations, particularly within the Gospels and Acts. Roman persecution in the first and second centuries intended to limit the practice of open preaching, or at least sought to suppress many records of it. Concerning second-century Christianity, E. Glenn Hinson suggested:

In this period as in the one before it, Christianity spread
chiefly through the sustained effort of organized Christian
communities . . . to win adherents. The typical convert
probably heard about Christianity by chance—a word
dropped by a friend or neighbor, witnessing a martyrdom,
overhearing a conversation—for, in time of persecution,
direct and open efforts to solicit members would have evoked
popular or governmental reaction and endangered the lives
of many persons.[13]

However, in his widely acclaimed *Evangelism in the Early Church*,
Michael Green's research led him to assert, "The challenge to
repentance and faith, coupled with the promises of joy and the
warnings of hell, are characteristic of second as much as of first
century Christian preaching."[14]

Hinson explained that ". . . over the first four or five centuries, the complex system of incorporation into the church
involved [multiple] distinct phases."[15] This multifaceted process
extended the interval of conversion, departing from the spontaneity observed in the New Testament. Such an approach intended
to ensure the Catholic Church's church membership remained
regenerate. Hinson further asserted, "Lengthy catechumenal
instruction [prior to baptism] sought to etch the lines of the covenant more sharply still."[16] Perhaps the impetus for the Catholic
Church's attempts to verify the authenticity of baptism candi-
dates' faith shares, to some extent, similarities with contemporary
concerns about the legitimacy of public gospel appeals for immediate decisions within evangelicalism. For example, evangelical
churches that delay baptizing newly professed believers usually
require them to undergo a modified form of catechesis, though
not always as formal or extensive as the previous catechumenal
instruction referenced earlier.

Hinson also noted that in the fourth century some like

Ambrose (339–397) and John Chrysostom (347–407) preached sermons in which they directly appealed for the conversion of their hearers.[17] Nevertheless, Roy Fish explained concerning the next twelve centuries:

> From the fifth century to the sixteenth century there is little evidence for evangelistic invitations being offered. This is due to a number of things. To begin with, vital evangelism was to a great degree dissipated. In a real sense, evangelism ceased to be evangelism. In many instances, because a king or tribal chief would be converted to the faith, the entire tribe would simultaneously become Christian. . . . Conversion became a matter of mass exercise, and ultimately infant baptism became prevalent in the church and conversion was assumed by the church with a later experience.[18]

These indigenous, leader-influenced "conversions" among pagan societies, as well as the birth of children into the magisterial Roman Church-State, diminished the practice of openly preaching for public, instantaneous decisions.

However, gospel invitations were still issued by some open-air preachers during the Middle Ages. For example, David Larsen asserted that Bernard of Clairvaux (1091?–1153) was known to ask hearers to indicate their responses to his preaching publicly by raising their hands.[19] Larsen also referenced Anthony of Padua's (1195?–1231) custom of starting with preaching and then lighting a bonfire so he could encourage those who possessed and played cards to cast them into the flames.[20] Other groups who preached the gospel and immediately baptized converts included the Waldensians and the Lollards.

As noted, Catholicism's sacramental system, in many cases, stymied the practice of first-century, immediate appeals for unbelievers to repent and believe. However, the Protestant

Reformation (1517–1648) recovered both the biblical gospel and the public preaching of it. As Martyn Lloyd-Jones declared, "The Reformers re-introduced preaching and put preaching at the center instead of ceremonies and sacraments."[21] Particularly, some of the Radical Reformers such as Balthasar Hubmaier (1480–1528), Conrad Grebel (1498–1526), Feliz Manz (1498–1527), and George Blaurock (1491–1529) opposed not only the sacramental system of the Church of Rome but also the infant baptisms practiced by the Magisterial Reformers. In contrast, they would call people to repent and believe. In fact, many of those who responded to the message the Radical Reformers preached were immediately re-"baptized" (for which they were known as Anabaptists) because their original magisterial baptism was not believer's baptism.

Although an altar call, specifically, cannot be traced from the inception of New Testament churches until today, forms of it were implemented long before Charles G. Finney used it. David Bennett even admitted in his critical study of the origins and present use of the altar call, "The public invitation would appear to have first been used sometime in the eighteenth century, yet it does not appear to have become systematized until early in the next."[22] For example, Eleazar Wheelock (1711–1779) was a congregational minister during the First Great Awakening. In October 1741 he preached in Lebanon, Connecticut, and multiple sources have reprinted an eyewitness's account of this meeting:

> As he was delivering his discourse very pleasantly and moderately, the depth and strength of feeling increased, till some began to cry out, both above and below, in awful distress and anguish of soul, upon which he raised his voice, that he might be heard above their outcries; but the distress and outcry spreading and increasing, his voice was at length so drowned that he could not be heard. *Wherefore, not being able to finish*

his sermon, with great apparent serenity and calmness of soul,
he called to the distressed, and desired them to gather themselves
together in the body of the seats below. This he did, that he might
the more conveniently converse with them, counsel, direct, exhort
them, etc.[23]

Additionally, William L. Lumpkin has documented activity akin to an altar call during the 1760s. He explained that the revival meetings conducted by the Sandy Creek tradition of Separate Baptists in North Carolina included the following:

At the close of the sermon, the minister would come down from the pulpit and while singing a suitable hymn would go around among the brethren shaking hands. The hymn being sung, he would then extend an invitation to such persons as felt themselves poor guilty sinners, and were anxiously inquiring the way of salvation, to come forward and kneel near the stand, or if they preferred, they could kneel at their seats, proffering to unite with them in prayer for their conversion.[24]

In the First Great Awakening, Jonathan Edwards (1703–1758), like his peers John Wesley (1703–1791) and George Whitefield (1714–1770), called for public, immediate decisions for Christ while preaching.[25] For example, in his sermon on Psalm 25:11, "Great Guilt No Obstacle to the Pardon of the Returning Sinner," Edwards declared, "The proper *use* of this subject is, to encourage sinners whose consciences are burdened with a sense of guilt, immediately to go to God through Christ for mercy. If you go in the manner we have described, the arms of mercy are open to embrace you."[26] Edwards also recounted sinners openly professing their faith in Christ when he defended the surprising work of God through conversion in Northampton, Massachusetts. In a letter to Benjamin Colman, a Boston pastor, he reported:

This dispensation has also appeared very extraordinary in the numbers of those on whom we have reason to hope it has had a saving effect. We have about six hundred and twenty communicants which include almost all our adult persons. The church was very large before; but persons never thronged into it as they did in the late extraordinary time. Our sacraments were eight weeks asunder, and *I received into our communion about a hundred before one sacrament, and four-score of them at one time, whose appearance, when they presented themselves together to make an open explicit profession of Christianity, was very affecting to the congregation. I took in near sixty before the next sacrament day; and I had very sufficient evidence of the conversion of their souls, through divine grace.*[27]

The nineteenth century also saw many examples of preachers publicly calling people to faith in Christ. Public appeals to receive the gospel were popularized through anxious benches, or altar calls, during the Second Great Awakening. Nathan Finn explains:

During the Second Great Awakening, frontier Methodists first used this practice in their camp meetings. Some Baptists in the South also adopted the practice, which they almost certainly learned from the Methodists, since these two groups frequently cooperated in camp meetings in the Carolinas and Georgia through the 1810s. In the 1820s and 1830s, Charles Finney popularized the view among Presbyterians, Congregationalists, and Baptists in the urban Northeast. Though he was accused of introducing "Methodist" practices among these more Calvinistic churches, altar calls (along with his other "new measures") became popular among many evangelicals.

> Though it is impossible to determine with certainty when altar calls became a part of the weekly liturgy of most . . . churches, the practice was common after the Civil War and nearly uniform by the early twentieth century.[28]

Since that time, public calls to Christian faith have included the preaching of Dwight L. Moody (1837–1899) and his inquiry room, Billy Sunday's (1862–1935) sawdust trail, and the evangelistic ministries of Sam Jones (1847–1906), R. A. Torrey (1856–1928), J. Wilbur Chapman (1859–1918), Rodney "Gipsy" Smith (1860–1947), Billy Graham (1918–2018), Luis Palau (1934–2021), and Greg Laurie (1952–), to name a few.

CONCLUSION

Preaching the gospel obliges ministers to issue public invitations to repent and to believe the gospel for several reasons. First, preachers in the Gospels and Acts predominately made disciples by publicly and immediately calling for unbelievers to repent of their sins and believe in Jesus Christ for salvation (e.g., Matt 3:2; 4:17; Mark 1:14–15; Acts 2:38; 3:19; 14:15; 26:20). Second, unbelievers who hear sermons do not know how to respond to the gospel apart from receiving instruction through an evangelistic invitation (e.g., Luke 3:10–14; Acts 2:37; 16:30). Third, the implicit nature of preaching itself anticipates that preachers will exhort their hearers to repent and believe in Christ. And, finally, preachers of the gospel have extended evangelistic appeals throughout the history of Christianity.

PLANNING PUBLIC GOSPEL INVITATIONS

INVITATIONS MATTER WHEN PEOPLE HEAR THE BIBLE preached. Because pastors cannot know the spiritual condition of everyone under the sound of their voices, they should include the gospel and its appeal in every sermon they preach. However, public gospel invitations never occur on accident—they are the result of intentional preparation. While numerous ministers spend time studying in order to develop their sermons and formulate their outlines, few of them include time to frame ways to exhort unbelievers directly from the text they plan to preach.

Reasons that explain why preachers exclude this aspect of their sermon preparation vary. One reason includes a sincere concern that direct exhortations may either infringe upon or demonstrate a lack of faith in the Holy Spirit's work to draw people to Christ. However, as Scott Pace has explained, "An unprepared invitation is not ultimately a matter of skill, spontaneity, or spiritual sensitivity. The Spirit's work is not synonymous with sermonic freelance, and to approach the invitation this way is spiritually irresponsible. He can be just as active in our study prior to the sermon as he is in the sanctuary at the end of it."[1] So long as preachers submit to the leading of the Spirit while they study, they can demonstrate cooperation with and confidence in Him to use prepared invitations to convince their hearers to receive Christ.

Many preachers have never considered or been taught how to utilize their sermon preparation time to craft their public call of people to faith in Christ from the Scripture passage they will preach. For this reason, this chapter practically explains how pastors, preachers, and evangelists can and should (1) pray for the Spirit to use their sermons to draw unbelievers to repentance and faith in Christ and (2) prepare their invitations to incorporate the inherent summons of the texts they preach. It concludes by providing a suggested prayer guide, as well as a step-by-step process by which those who prepare sermons are able to identify and articulate the gospel summons in each text they preach.

PLANNING YOUR GOSPEL INVITATIONS THROUGH PRAYER

In order to pray effectively for the lost, preachers and the churches in which they minister must grasp a basic, scriptural understanding of why an unbeliever is without Christ in the first place. Behind the simple fact that the lost person has not received the gospel is the reality that he or she is not only bound but also blinded by "the god of this world," Satan. In the words of the apostle Paul, Christians should pray that lost men and women might "come to their senses and escape from the snare of the devil, after being captured by him to do his will" (2 Tim 2:26). In praying for others during times of appeal, pastors should be aware that in this battle unbelievers are bound and blinded.

Paul also says, "And even if our gospel is veiled, it is veiled to those who are perishing. In their case the god of this world has blinded the minds of the unbelievers, to keep them from seeing the light of the gospel of the glory of Christ, who is the image of God" (2 Cor 4:3–4). Thus, two things need to happen before a person can be saved: the binding and the blinding must be broken. This spiritual freedom occurs only through intercession: "For the weapons of our warfare are not of the flesh but have divine power to destroy strongholds. We destroy arguments and every lofty opinion raised against the knowledge of God, and take every thought captive to obey Christ" (2 Cor 10:4–5).

Thus, Christians have the power in prayer to move into the spiritual realm and knock down the stronghold in which the devil has a lost person bound and blinded. Consequently, those who pray at the time of appeal should not direct their efforts to a particular individual—but at the devil himself. This is what the Lord did in Caesarea Philippi. After Jesus instructed the disciples about His ensuing death, Peter, with good intentions, sought to divert Him from the cross. Jesus curtly replied, "Get behind me, Satan!" (Matt 16:23) He was not addressing Himself to Peter, because He realized the devil was the power behind Peter motivating him to say what he had said. Thus, Jesus dealt directly with the devil.

Paul followed Christ's example when, upon being "greatly annoyed" by a slave girl who had a spirit of divination, he "turned and said to the spirit, 'I command you in the name of Jesus Christ to come out of her'" (Acts 16:18b). Prayer is clearly the true battlefield in "the valley of decision" when people are weighing their ultimate destiny in the balance of eternity. The task of Christians as intercessors, when the appeal is being extended, is to "destroy strongholds" (2 Cor 10:4), which are the binding and the blinding that keep men and women from a saving knowledge of Christ. After all, "no one can enter a strong man's house and plunder his goods, unless he first binds the strong man" (Mark 3:27).

As pastors extend the gospel invitation, intercessors should simultaneously be praying and demolishing demonic strongholds. When a public appeal is extended during corporate worship, preachers and members of the congregation should be mindful of what is going on in the unseen world around them. A battle is being waged for the souls of men and women who sit in the church.

For this reason, prayer must be a priority when drawing the net. Pastors should instruct their congregations to pray for and demolish three primary strongholds. The first of these strongholds is *pride*. Pride, the *big I*, the perpendicular pronoun, keeps more people from responding to Jesus Christ than anything else. Those in this stronghold are more concerned about what others think than what God thinks.

A second stronghold to pray against is *presumption*. Some do not respond to the gospel appeal because they are presuming upon some "decision" made years ago that resulted in no transformation of life. Many people trapped in this stronghold thus needlessly enter a Christless eternity.

The other major stronghold to demolish in prayer is *procrastination*. Some think there will be adequate time in the future to respond to the gospel, so they postpone the call. They keep putting it off. When people are freed from this stronghold, they then realize that not to decide *is* to decide.

Pastors should desire an army of prayer warriors who pray for the demolition of strongholds in every service. They should teach members of their congregation personally to identify an individual in the congregation at the beginning of worship and pray for him or her during the entire service. Mobilizing a congregation into praying for the salvation of unbelievers who attend worship services requires that the pastor should train them to pray in such a way that does not distract them from being edified by God's Word and the Holy Spirit. The pastor may want to establish a rotation system of prayer warriors who are assigned one Sunday over an interval of time (e.g., once a month, once a quarter, or once a year) to pray in a designated intercessory room that livestreams the worship service. Another example includes training congregants to identify a particular point made in the sermon and briefly pray that God will use it to convict the unbeliever about his or her sin. Also, petitioners could pray inconspicuously while they stand during the song of response, or they can pray for the salvation of the unbeliever kneeling at the altar, if an altar call is being used.

PLANNING YOUR GOSPEL INVITATIONS THROUGH SERMON PREPARATION

Every preacher's sermon preparation should include a designated effort to craft an invitation that flows out of the textual idea of each particular passage. The inherent nature of both the Scriptures and the gospel elicits a response on the part of those who hear it. As D. Martyn Lloyd-Jones wrote concerning a preacher's appeal for decisions at the close of his sermon:

> My . . . argument is that the preaching of the Word and the call for decision should not be separated in our thinking. That calls for further explanation. . . .
>
> My contention is that . . . the tendency increasingly has been to put more and more emphasis on the "appeal" and the taking of a decision, and to regard it as something in and of itself. I remember being in an evangelistic meeting in which I, and others, felt that on that occasion the Gospel had not really been preached. It had been mentioned, but it

certainly had not been conveyed, it had not been preached; but to my amazement a large number of people went forward in response to the appeal at the end. The question that arose immediately was, what accounted for this? I was discussing this question the following day with a friend. He said, "There is no difficulty about that, '[*sic*] these results have nothing to do with the preaching." So I asked, "Well, what is it, what was happening?" He replied, "This is God answering the prayers of the thousands of people who are praying for these results throughout the world; it is not the preaching." My contention is that there should be no such disjunction between the "appeal" and the preaching.[2]

Furthermore, effective text-driven preachers who call sinners to salvation in Jesus Christ alone by faith in Him alone should not tack on generic and weekly repetitive invitations to the end of their sermons. For example, numerous preachers who extend a public invitation usually say something like this: "Today, I call you to Christ. I call you to salvation. I invite you to come and inquire about how to join this church family." However, imagine how their calls for sinners to repent and believe Christ would sound if these invitations naturally flow from their text's genre and immediate application.

Invitations that emanate from the textual idea of the passage preached require preparation on the part of preachers. A four-step process can assist them in composing and articulating public appeals in their sermons for unbelievers to repent and believe the gospel. This process requires ministers to (1) classify the genre of the text they intend to preach; (2) associate the gospel message with the text they have selected to preach; (3) identify spiritual needs and/or problems present within the text; and (4) compose a gospel exhortation that anticipates the lost who will hear them preach their text.

STEP ONE: CLASSIFY THE GENRE OF YOUR TEXT

First, you should identify the genre of the passage you have selected to preach. Doing so enables you to determine how you can instruct your hearers to apply and/or receive the textual solution to their spiritual deficiencies. In his book *Recapturing the Voice of God*, Steven Smith has identified nine genres within the Scriptures: (1) Old Testament Narrative; (2) Law; (3) Psalms; (4) Prophecy; (5) Wisdom Literature; (6) Gospels/Acts; (7) Parables; (8) Epistles; and (9) Apocalyptic. Smith condenses these into three general categories:

1. STORY (NARRATIVE): Old Testament Narrative, Law, Gospels/Acts, Parables
2. POEM: Psalms, Prophecy, Wisdom Literature
3. LETTER: Epistles, Apocalyptic[3]

In fact, Smith contended that "the genres of Scripture are not things that need to be willfully bent toward Christ by the preacher; rather, they exist like they do *because* of the gospel message."[4] Thus, recognizing the literary genre of the text will help ensure your invitation is consistent with the spirit—or the authorial intent—of the passage.

STEP TWO: ASSOCIATE THE GOSPEL WITH YOUR TEXT

Second, you should discern the natural connection between the gospel and the textual idea of the Scripture passage you will preach—that is, you need to see both the divine and human authors' intended purpose and meaning for writing it. As Steven Smith correctly claimed, "The nature of Scripture gives warrant to the idea of preaching Christ from any Scripture—or more precisely, showing how all Scripture advances the plan of the gospel of which Christ is operative and through which he will be exalted."[5] Your text's genre classification, as determined from the previous step, will assist you in associating its textual idea with innate cues that point toward the gospel's benefits. Therefore, when you preach a **story** or narrative (e.g., an Old Testament Narrative, the Law, a Gospel/Acts, or a Parable), first identify either the sin problem or righteousness example presented in the text's narration. Then, call on those struggling with that particular sin, or falling short in that area of righteousness, to accept and apply the gospel's remedy for them.

If the passage you plan to preach is a **poem** (e.g., Psalms, Prophecy, or Wisdom Literature), associate the text's *confession, recollection,* and *promise* with the ways in which the gospel pertains to those themes. In terms of texts that consist of a *confession,* the Psalms and some of the Wisdom Literature regularly express the author's candid acknowledgment of needing to be forgiven of his sins, protected from evil, or advised to reject folly and fault. Therefore, associate the gospel with the *confession.* Instruct your hearers to acknowledge their need for God's forgiveness, protection, and counsel so they can become righteous through faith in Christ. In relation to passages that contain a *recollection,* the Psalms and some prophetic literature recall times when God saved His people from imminent danger and threats. Describe how the gospel relates to *recollection* in that it instructs unbelievers of God's mighty power to save those who trust in Him alone. Concerning Scriptures that entail a *promise,* the Psalms and Prophecy genres both contain prophe cies of God's Anointed One who will bring about His salvation and His reign. When preaching such texts, ensure you correlate the gospel with the *promise* by citing the messianic prophecies concerning Christ and pointing to evidence of their fulfillment in the New Testament.

If preaching a **letter** or instruction passage (e.g., Epistles or Apocalyptic), ascertain how the text's teaching connects with the gospel's instruction for unbelievers to repent and receive the gospel's power to enable their obedience. Or, when preaching an Apocalyptic passage, appeal to how the gospel provides an eternal way of escape from the judgment to come. Examples of gospel associations in sample textual genres are found in the conclusion of this chapter in *Step Two* of "Examples of How to Craft the Invitation of Your Sermon."

The Scriptures are sufficient to save sinners. When you determine the association between your passage's textual idea and the gospel, in the context of its genre, your invitation becomes a beneficiary of the power and authority of Scripture's sufficiency to save. Instead of tacking a monotonous and repetitive invitational script on the end of your sermon, utilize the powerful thrust of the very Scripture you preached and bear witness to its sufficiency to convict, rebuke, and convince sinners to accept the gospel.

STEP THREE: IDENTIFY THE SPIRITUAL NEEDS AND/OR PROBLEMS WITHIN YOUR TEXT

Third, identify the spiritual needs and/or problems people are facing within the text you are preaching, which only the gospel can remedy. These needs and problems consist of deficiencies that result from people rejecting God and/or His gospel. For example, they can be located in the Scriptures when the following characteristics are observed:

1. Benefits that only the righteous can access;
2. Consequences resulting from sinful actions or behaviors;
3. Questions or pleas that disobedient people pose to God or the righteous; and
4. Pronouncements upon or against the wicked by prophets, including rebukes, curses, indictments, or divinations.

See three specific examples of spiritual needs/problems in the conclusion of this chapter under *Step Three* of "Examples of How to Craft the Invitation of Your Sermon."

STEP FOUR: ARTICULATE THE GOSPEL EXHORTATION OF YOUR TEXT

Finally, compile your work from the previous three steps in order to compose the gospel exhortation of the passage of Scripture you will preach. A preacher must not be content merely to impart knowledge and facts about the text he preaches; he must also endeavor to use that knowledge and those facts to exhort his hearers to repent and believe. Urging unbelievers to receive the gospel from the very verses preached to them requires you to contextualize the spiritual needs and/or problems you found within your sermon's text into *profile descriptions* of similar needs/problems that match those of unbelievers you anticipate will hear your sermon. Three examples of how to compose *profile descriptions* are found at the conclusion of this chapter in *Step Four* of "Examples of How to Craft the Invitation of Your Sermon."

Next, locate the inherent *gospel exhortation* of your text so that the Scripture itself forms the particular invitation you offer your hearers. Pastor Josh Smith offers the following questions to assist preachers in comprehending the exhortation of the text they preach:

1. What is the direct command of the text?
2. What was the original application of the text?
3. What is the need of the audience [to whom you preach]?[6]

Likewise, Southeastern Baptist Theological Seminary president Danny Akin suggests that preachers ask thirteen questions of each passage they preach so that they can locate and identify its gospel exhortation:

1. Is there an example for me to follow?
2. Is there a sin to avoid/confess?
3. Is there a promise to claim?
4. Is there a prayer to repeat?
5. Is there a command to obey?
6. Is there a condition to meet?
7. Is there a verse to memorize?
8. Is there an error to avoid?
9. Is there a challenge to face?
10. Is there a principle to apply?
11. Is there a habit to change—that is, start or stop?
12. Is there an attitude to correct?
13. Is there a truth to believe?[7]

Finally, compose specific *gospel exhortations* by which you or a decision encourager can transition into instructing unbelievers how to become baptized, obedient disciples of Jesus Christ. Basically, *exhortations* articulate how unbelievers who identify with specific, spiritual needs/problems can have them met by accepting the gospel. They also provide precise and direct instruction on how sinners can repent of their sins and believe in Christ alone for their salvation. Three examples of how to compose *gospel exhortations* are found at the conclusion of this chapter in *Step Four* of "Examples of How to Craft the Invitation of Your Sermon."

Utilize key words from the passage in your articulation of the *profile description* and the *gospel exhortation*. While every *profile description* and *gospel exhortation* may be incorporated into the delivery of your sermon, you should not feel required to use all of them. However, a sufficient number of these must purposefully be presented throughout your sermon so that your hearers realize they have a consequential decision to make—either to receive or to reject the gospel of Jesus Christ. They should not leave the service indifferent and unaware of their responsibility to receive the forgiveness of sins and to be reconciled with God through Christ.

CONCLUSION

Sermon preparation requires more than consulting respectable commentaries, crafting engaging illustrations, and constructing your sermon's points. It includes intentionally praying for the salvation of unbelievers who will hear your sermon, as well as crafting an invitation that communicates the summons of the text you preach. The following two exercises provide a step-by-step process that will assist you in (1) praying for unbelievers who will hear your sermon and (2) preparing the invitation you will extend at the conclusion of your sermon.

EXERCISE ONE: A GUIDE TO PRAY FOR UNBELIEVERS WHO WILL HEAR YOUR SERMON

In order to make prayerful preparations for unbelievers who will hear the next sermon you will preach, do the following:

a. List the names of unbelievers that you expect will come and hear you preach your sermon. The people you identify in order to compose this list of names might include the following: unregenerate church members; regularly attending unbelieving guests; the unbelieving children and students of church members; those whom you and your congregants have personally evangelized over the last week; people you and your congregants have personally invited to attend the church; and unsaved family members and friends who may attend a baptism, a holiday celebration (e.g., Easter and Christmas), or a special recognition/performance of members of your church (e.g., graduation acknowledgment, Vacation Bible School celebration, children's or student's musical, etc.).

_____

_____

_____

b. Write the name of each unbeliever after the specific strongholds mentioned earlier—*pride, presumption,* and/or procrastination— that the Word and the Spirit must overcome in them so that they may repent and believe.
PRIDE: _____
PRESUMPTION: _____
PROCRASTINATION: _____

c. List the names of believers in your church and assign each of them one of the unbelievers' names. Ask them to pray for the salvation of the person they were assigned throughout the week and during the service. Use the material from earlier in this chapter to instruct them how to pray for the destruction of their assigned unbeliever's stronghold, so that he or she may repent and believe in Christ.

_____

_____

_____

d. List the names of other believers in your church whom you can mobilize to pray during the service(s) in which you preach. Ask them to pray for the salvation of unbelievers not named in this exercise, those who will also hear the gospel and be asked to respond in repentance and faith.

_____

_____

_____

EXERCISE TWO: EXAMPLES OF HOW TO CRAFT THE
INVITATION OF YOUR SERMON

Utilize the four steps outlined earlier in this chapter when
preparing how you will articulate your sermon's exhortation.
Example texts (e.g., Ps 1:1–6; Mark 10:17–22; Eph 2:1–9) have
been selected to illustrate how to apply these four steps when
crafting your invitation:

> *Step One:* Classify which of the three categorical genres—
> *Poem*, *Story*, or *Letter*—best describes the passage of
> Scripture you will preach.

Example Texts
    Psalm 1:1–6
        Poem Genre

    Mark 10:17–22
        Story Genre

    Ephesians 2:1–9
        Letter Genre

> *Step Two:* Identify specific ways or cues that the textual
> idea of the Scripture passage you will preach relates to the
> gospel.

Poem Genre Example (Psalm 1:1–6)

THE GOSPEL PROVIDES:	OUR SIN AND WICKEDNESS:
blessing (v. 1)	prevents blessing (v. 4a)
stability (v. 3)	produces instability (v. 5)
prosperous living (v. 3d)	results in perishing (v. 6b)

Story Genre Example (Mark 10:17–22)

In reply to the young man, Jesus answers the most important question that could ever be asked: "What must I do to inherit eternal life?" (v. 17).

Letter Genre Example (Ephesians 2:1–9)

GRACE THROUGH FAITH:	OUR TRESPASSES, TRANSGRESSIONS, AND SINS:
makes us alive (v. 5b)	make us dead (vv. 1, 5a)
saves us (vv. 5c, 8)	enslave us (v. 2)
raises us (vv. 6–7)	debase us (v. 3)

> *Step Three:* Using the gospel cues identified in *Step Two*, locate and articulate the spiritual needs and/or spiritual problems present in the passage of Scripture you will preach, which only the gospel can solve.

Poem Genre Example (Psalm 1:1–6)

The spiritual needs and/or spiritual problems in this passage that relate to unbelievers include:

a. needing God's blessing (v. 1);
b. needing freedom from sinful company (v. 1);
c. needing stability (vv. 3–4);
d. needing a prosperous life—that is, abundant life/life to the full (v. 3d);
e. needing access to God and the righteous (v. 5); and
f. needing to be rescued from perishing (v. 6b).

Story Genre Example (Mark 10:17–22)

The spiritual needs and/or spiritual problems in this passage that relate to unbelievers include:

a. a desire for eternal life (v. 17d);
b. a failure to confess Jesus as God (vv. 17c–18, 20a);
c. a commitment to moral living without revering God (vv. 19–20b); and
d. a sinful fidelity to possessions over God (vv. 21–22).

Letter Genre Example (Ephesians 2:1–9)

The spiritual needs and/or spiritual problems in this passage that relate to unbelievers include:

a. walking in the path of disobedience and in the company of the disobedient (vv. 2–3);
b. indulging in the desires of the flesh and the mind (v. 3b);
c. being condemned under the wrath of God (v. 3c);
d. working for one's own salvation (v. 9); and
e. needing God's mercy, great love, and kindness (vv. 4, 7).

Step Four: Contextualize the spiritual needs and/or spiritual problems identified in *Step Three* into *profile descriptions* of unbelievers who will hear you preach this passage of Scripture. Then compose specific *gospel exhortations* by which you or a decision encourager can instruct them how to become baptized, obedient disciples of Jesus Christ. Utilize as many key words as you can from the passage in your articulation of the *profile description* and the *gospel exhortation.*

Poem Genre Example (Psalm 1:1–6)

a. PROFILE DESCRIPTION OF THOSE IN NEED OF GOD'S BLESSING: Some of you here today stand in need of God's blessing. You feel as if God is against you at every turn. Your life is restless and without peace.

GOSPEL EXHORTATION: At this very moment God's blessing and His peace are available to you, if you will only repent of your sins and place your faith in Jesus Christ. I invite you to receive Him now!

b. PROFILE DESCRIPTION OF THOSE NEEDING TO BREAK AWAY FROM SINFUL COMPANY: Some of you have been running with the wrong crowd. They have brought you nothing but pain and problems; you keep giving, and they just keep taking. You have been longing for a relationship with someone who will build you up instead of tearing you down.

GOSPEL EXHORTATION: I would like to introduce you to Someone who will never let you down. He will neither leave you nor forsake you. He is Someone who needs nothing from you, but you need everything from Him. His name is Jesus, and you must receive Him by faith today!

c. **PROFILE DESCRIPTION OF THOSE WHO NEED STABILITY:** Someone here today may feel as if his or her life is falling apart. Every time you try and stand on your own two feet, you get knocked right back down; you just cannot get a foothold in life. You feel that the winds of life are blowing against you so hard that you just cannot move in the right direction.

GOSPEL EXHORTATION: Right now God offers you the stability you so desperately desire. In order to receive it, you must turn away from your sins and place your complete trust in Jesus Christ to forgive you and plant your feet on solid ground.

d. **PROFILE DESCRIPTION OF THOSE IN NEED OF A PROSPEROUS LIFE:** Does it seem that everything you do is wrong? You give life your best effort, but you neither prosper nor flourish. Does anyone here feel as though life is empty—just a great big void? Has the devil just continued to steal, kill, and destroy any chance of hope you thought you had?

GOSPEL EXHORTATION: Today, you must change your way of thinking and realize that despite your best efforts, you cannot please God. However, Jesus died, was buried, and was raised from the dead in order to offer you full and abundant life. He alone pleases God—and if you will place your faith in Him, He will give you life in the here and now, as well as life in the hereafter.

e. PROFILE DESCRIPTION OF THOSE NEEDING ACCESS TO GOD AND THE RIGHTEOUS: Does someone here feel cut off from God? Do you sense the love of God when you are around His children and long for what they have?

GOSPEL EXHORTATION: God is not far from you. He is here, this very moment, and He bids you to turn to Him. Right now, you can be the recipient of His love by becoming His child through a personal relationship with His Son, Jesus Christ.

f. PROFILE DESCRIPTION OF THOSE NEEDING TO BE RESCUED FROM PERISHING: Some of you in this room are on a road to ruin. If you were to die right now, you know your sin would cause you to perish forever in hell. Today, you realize that God's Word provides for you a way to escape the impending torment that awaits you.

GOSPEL EXHORTATION: Today, I call you to change your way of living. Turn from your sin and to the Savior. Receive Him through repentance and faith right now.

Story Genre Example (Mark 10:17–22)

a. PROFILE DESCRIPTION OF THOSE WHO DESIRE OR HAVE QUESTIONS ABOUT ETERNAL LIFE: Someone in our midst today has been thinking about life after death. You have been searching and asking, "What can I do to have assurance about life after death?"

GOSPEL EXHORTATION: Just as He did with this young man in our text, Jesus offers you eternal life. In order to receive Him, you must decide to follow Him now. Will you come today and speak with someone so you will know how to follow Jesus?

b. **PROFILE DESCRIPTION OF THOSE WHO HAVE NOT GENUINELY CONFESSED JESUS AS THEIR LORD:** Has someone here today realized that when you prayed to ask Jesus into your heart at a younger age, that you only went through the motions and did not sincerely mean it? Have you been putting your faith in that prayer all this time instead of believing in Jesus Christ alone for your salvation?

GOSPEL EXHORTATION: Today, you can receive Christ by faith by calling on His name. The Bible tells us, "Everyone who calls on the name of the Lord will be saved" (Rom 10:13). Won't you come speak with one of the encouragers here at the front or at the welcome center at the end of the service and learn how to confess Jesus as your Lord by believing in Him?

c. **PROFILE DESCRIPTION OF THOSE WHO VALUE LIVING A MORAL LIFE ABOVE REVERING GOD:** A number of you today have been trying to please God by keeping the Ten Commandments and being a good person. However, this encounter between Jesus and the young man has caused you to realize that your attempts to satisfy God in this way fail miserably. In fact, they offend Him. Any attempt to appease God apart from completely trusting in the only One who has ever pleased the Father—Jesus Christ—communicates to God that His Son's death, burial, and resurrection for your sins is not sufficient to save you.

GOSPEL EXHORTATION: Will you stop trusting in yourself and the things that you have done, and place your complete trust in Jesus Christ alone for your salvation?

d. PROFILE DESCRIPTION OF THOSE WHO VALUE THEIR POSSESSIONS OVER GOD: What is standing between you and God? Do you have control over your possessions, or do they control you?

GOSPEL EXHORTATION: Today, Jesus calls you to lay aside those things that you value more than Him and follow Him. I invite you to speak with an encourager today, who can assist you in surrendering the things that stand between you and a personal relationship with Jesus Christ.

Letter Genre Example (Ephesians 2:1–9)

a. PROFILE DESCRIPTION OF THOSE WHO WALK IN THE PATH OF DISOBEDIENCE AND IN THE COMPANY OF THE DISOBEDIENT: Who among us here today finds themselves on the highway to destruction? You know you are going in the wrong direction, but today's Scripture has awakened you to the fact that you need to exit this path quickly. You have been walking in the power of the Evil One instead of being directed by God's Holy Spirit.

GOSPEL EXHORTATION: Today, Christ offers you a way of escape from the path upon which you find yourself. He offers you freedom from the grip of the devil if you will turn away from the path you're on and place your complete trust in Him to save you.

b. PROFILE DESCRIPTION OF THOSE WHO INDULGE IN THE DESIRES OF THE FLESH AND THE MIND: Some of you today continually indulge and yield to your fleshly impulses. You know it's wrong, but you feel as though you just cannot stop. Your body and mind are engaging in activities that betray the purpose for which God gave them to you.

GOSPEL EXHORTATION: Right now, Jesus calls you to break free from the influence that your primal desires have over your body and mind. He freely offers you a renewed heart to control these desires. Will you invite Him to take residence in your heart today as Lord of your life?

c. **PROFILE DESCRIPTION OF THOSE CONDEMNED UNDER THE WRATH OF GOD:** I am convinced that some of you today sense God's anger and wrath against you and your sin. You feel embarrassed for what you've done, and the guilt and shame of your sin are overwhelming you right now. Perhaps you are questioning if you can escape God's righteous gaze that seems to penetrate right through you.

GOSPEL EXHORTATION: Jesus Christ, who was fully God and fully man, hung upon the cross to absorb God's wrath and anger against your sins. He was buried, and then He was raised from the dead on the third day so that today when God looks at you, He sees Jesus's righteousness and not your unrighteousness. Will you receive Christ by faith right now?

d. **PROFILE DESCRIPTION OF THOSE WHO ATTEMPT TO WORK FOR THEIR OWN SALVATION:** Many religious people have convinced themselves that they can earn their own salvation by doing good things and refraining from doing bad things. Trying to please God on this basis can be tiring. It also leads to frustration because you are constantly weighing your good works against your bad ones. However, your bad will always outweigh your good, and the only way for you to gain salvation is to abandon those deceptive scales and turn to the dependable Savior.

GOSPEL EXHORTATION: If you were to save yourself, then you would certainly take credit for it. However, salvation by God's free gift of grace through faith is not of works, so you and I are unable to brag about it. Only Jesus's work on the cross can save sinners—so, will you trust in Him today?

e. **PROFILE DESCRIPTION OF THOSE IN NEED OF GOD'S MERCY, GREAT LOVE, AND KINDNESS:** Someone under the sound of my voice likely stands in need of God's mercy, love, and kindness. You realize you are under deep conviction for every sinful thing you have ever done, and you deeply desire God's goodness to replace the shame and guilt you feel.

GOSPEL EXHORTATION: As we have seen in our text, God's mercy is abundant, and He loves us greatly. Today, the kindness of the Savior is extended freely to you. Will you receive God's mercy, love, and kindness today through faith in Christ alone?

EXTENDING PUBLIC GOSPEL INVITATIONS

PREACHING TEXTBOOKS AND CLASSES GENERALLY FAIL TO provide tutorials for issuing public gospel invitations that students can confidently replicate. This chapter provides much-needed instruction on clear and effective ways to offer gospel invitations. It shows preachers how to avoid using repetitive tags at the end of their sermons and teaches them how to incorporate the textual idea of the Scripture they preach to drive the public call to faith.

EXTENDING THE GOSPEL INVITATION WITH ENGAGING POSTURE

A number of preachers extend altar calls as a legitimate form of issuing gospel invitations. After stepping down from the platform and assuming a position in the center of the aisle, some immediately bow their heads and close their eyes in prayer for people to respond. Such pleas for God to save sinners are noble. However, people in the audience are less likely to approach the praying minister because they fear they will interrupt his talking with God.

The devil will try and use anything he can—even prayer in this case—to provide unbelievers an excuse not to accept Christ. For this reason, those who find themselves praying in this manner should consider exercising one of two suggested options. In the first option, the minister can pray for the lost to respond to the invitation either before the worship service begins or during the congregational singing before his message. Then he, having appealed to God and his audience, should fix his eyes upon the people with expectant faith that some will come. Alternatively, if the minister feels a strong conviction to pray during the invitation, he should do so with his eyes open.

Another consideration relating to the preacher's posture when he extends an invitation to receive the gospel involves his body language. As much as he may desire that people respond, he may not have seen such instances for a long time. In such situations, the preacher's mannerisms might subconsciously reflect his doubts that this time will be any different than the ones before. The preacher may communicate an unintended expectancy for people to respond by looking at his watch, staring at the clock in the back of the worship center, looking down, frowning, shifting his weight to one side, putting his hands on his hips, or crossing his arms restrictively. In order to avert such unintentional body language, he should consider intentionally avoiding the aforementioned tics by smiling, scanning the congregation while briefly looking into individuals' eyes, and perhaps extending a welcome invitation to join him by opening his arms or hand toward the audience.

EXTENDING THE GOSPEL
INVITATION PLAINLY

Words are important. In issuing Christ's appeal preachers must articulate their words in language that unchurched people can understand, since many unbelievers have not been exposed to Christian environments. Preachers communicate every week to people who may have not been inside a church since childhood or who may never have entered an evangelical church. And several public appeals fail to elicit a response simply because the hearers are uncertain about what they are being challenged to do.

Picture that man or woman in church for the first time. The pastor comes to the end of his sermon by announcing, "We will now turn to hymn number 240. Will you come?" Though all the "old-timers" know what the pastor means, the very person he is trying to reach begins to ask several questions. *Come to whom? Why? Come for what? When? Where?* Many pastors cast the net in this way, but they never draw it in because they assume the hearers understand what is required. However, many of those hearers simply do not comprehend the preacher's words, so plain language is imperative.

Consider young adults who have no church background or biblical training. Many do not know that Matthew, Mark, Luke, and John are books of the Bible. Some have been reared in homes where they have never heard a prayer and have never seen the Bible open. In striving to impact new generations for Christ, we need to know how to think as non-Christians think. In this way, those who publicly proclaim the Word can speak plainly to reach people whose main question about the faith is not so much, "Is it true?" but "Is it relevant?" They want to know, "Does it fit?"—"Is it what I need?"—"Does it speak to me?"

Before he ever speaks, the pastor should consider the

perspectives of his hearers and have a clear idea of what he wants them to know and do. In addition, he should be able to explain *why* they should act. The pastor should seek to present a plain appeal, assuming nothing about the hearer's knowledge. Though this plain appeal may require additional time at the conclusion of the sermon, it will helpfully include practical information about *when, where,* and *how* a person should respond (for example, "stand up, step into the aisle, and make your way to the front"). The pastor should make his hearers aware that when they respond this way they are saying, *"I am going Christ's way today."* Those responding to the appeal should be assured that they do not have to worry about what to say when they reach the front because their act of courage testifies, "I want to know Christ today." As they give an invitation to respond, effective ministers will make their message and the process plain so that no surprises occur.

EXTENDING THE GOSPEL INVITATION POSITIVELY

A *positive* appeal does not refer to some hyped-up, pumped-up mental attitude. Rather, it means that the preacher has solid, positive confidence built and based upon faith in the promises found in God's Word. Many people unfortunately never respond to public appeals because those appeals are so void of optimism and expectancy. Consequently, pastors can positively frame their appeals by saying something like, *"I believe many are going to come to receive the gift of eternal life and find a new beginning, and you are going to join them. You have thought about it, prayed about it, and even planned on it—and the only thing left is just to do it! You be first. Do not wait on anyone else. This is the right thing to do."* Expectancy and optimism thus become atmospheric and contagious.

The main reason so many see so little fruit is that they do not expect anything to happen. Many preachers are too timid at the "net-drawing" time because they fear failure, so they fall into manipulation or seek to shame the hearers by scolding, berating, or bullying them. In contrast, productive appeals are positive appeals exuding from a countenance of optimism and expectancy.

EXTENDING THE GOSPEL INVITATION PERSONALLY

One of the most personal life decisions is making a conscious choice to become a follower of the Lord Jesus Christ. The one making the appeal to trust in Christ must be sensitive to this personal dynamic.

The types of pronouns used in making an appeal reveal much about how speakers perceive their relationships with hearers. For example, ministers with a strong sense of identity and compassion for their people frequently speak in terms of "we" and "us." Though the most aloof are prone to speak more in terms of "they" or "them," those with exalted opinions of themselves too frequently punctuate their appeals with the perpendicular pronoun "I," along with "me" and "mine."

Most preaching today is in the first-person plural or the third-person plural. That is, preachers use plenty of "we" and "they" in their public proclamations—but this kind of preaching seldom produces conviction. Nothing is wrong with preaching in the first- and third-person voice, but gospel preachers are obliged to apply the textual idea of what they are preaching, allowing the invitation to flow out of the substance of the message. In this critical moment the one making the appeal needs to move from first and third person to second person—from "we" and "they" to "you." Furthermore, this "you" is not a second-person plural, but a second-person singular. This approach emphasizes the moment of challenge to each hearer, the hinge of the entire gospel appeal. Some today may settle into the comfort of first- and third-person appeals because they are afraid of offending their hearers with such a confrontational approach. No wonder many churches have such little power today; gospel appeals must be personal.

A quick look at the first recorded appeals of Simon Peter (Acts 2) and the apostle Paul (Acts 13) reveal an important insight for preachers today. When "drawing the net," they moved from first- and third-person pronouns to second-person pronouns at the critical point of their appeals. Consider Simon Peter as he stood on the Temple Mount in Jerusalem: "This Jesus, delivered up according to the definite plan and foreknowledge of God, *you* crucified and killed by the hands of lawless men" (2:23, emphasis added). Likewise, listen to the apostle Paul in the synagogue at Antioch: "Let it be known to *you* therefore, brothers, that through this man forgiveness of sins is proclaimed to *you*" (13:38, emphasis added).

The proclamation of the good news must appeal to the whole person. Like Peter and Paul, Christians should aim not merely at the head but also the heart. This type of appeal convicts the very being of the hearers; they are deeply moved. For example, after Peter finished his appeal, the Bible reports, "Now when they heard this they were cut to the heart" (2:37).

As mentioned earlier, when ministers invite people to become followers of Christ, they are asking them to make the most personal decision they will ever make in their lifetime. Consider how a life insurance agent makes his appeal: he does not speak in terms of what "they" should do or what "we" should do. He makes his presentation, and then he lays it on the line: "Now, here is what you should do to secure your family's future." All successful salesmen deal in second-person pronouns. How much more should those who appeal to the lost adopt this approach, so that their hearers may receive the gift of God, eternal life through Jesus Christ our Lord, accompanied by the forgiveness of sins?

EXTENDING THE GOSPEL
INVITATION PRESSINGLY

Calling men and women to faith in Christ should be done with persistence and a sense of urgency, because it is indeed the most urgent work in the world.

After Peter finished his message at Pentecost, the Bible records that "with many other words he bore witness and continued to exhort them" (Acts 2:40). Peter was pressing for a decision from his hearers. The word translated as *exhort* is derived from a Greek verb that means "to beseech with strong force" or "to call forth." Throughout the Bible we find people pressing their hearers to come to a decision. When Moses descended from Mount Sinai to find his people worshiping the golden calf, he drew the line with them, saying, "Whoever is on the LORD's side—come to me" (Exod 32:26 NKJV). When Joshua came to the end of his life, he gathered the people together and pressed them for a decision: "Choose this day whom you will serve. . . . As for me . . . [I] will serve the LORD" (Josh 24:15). Elijah, standing tall on Mount Carmel, pressed the people to decide for the Lord, asking, "How long will you falter between two opinions? If the LORD is God, follow Him" (1 Kgs 18:21 NKJV). The apostle Paul framed his appeal to the Corinthians in this way: "We are ambassadors for Christ, God making his appeal through us. We implore you on behalf of Christ, be reconciled to God" (2 Cor 5:20).

This word describing the urgency of pleading a cause is illustrated in what happened at the Alamo in 1836. The Texans holed up in the Alamo were facing certain death and trying to "buy time" for General Sam Houston's forces to assemble near what is now Houston. General Santa Anna's Mexican army had been besieging the Alamo for some time and was now preparing for the final assault. As the story goes, Colonel William B. Travis gathered his men in the courtyard on that fateful night. With his sword, he drew a line in the sand and challenged those who would stay with him and fight for the cause to cross over the line. It was a calling to one's side. The rest is history.

The model appeal of Peter was urgent and persistent in beseeching his hearers—with strong force—to come to Christ's side. In the Pentecostal appeal Peter did not issue the call, sit down, and look humble. He did not finish his sermon and suggest, *"Now, let's sing a hymn. If by chance there is anyone here who would like to stand for Christ, you may do so at this time. But please do not feel like you must."* Neither did he say, *"Now, if you want to make a decision, you may meet with the elders of the church,"* nor, *"You may meet with our membership committee next month."* Peter did not apologize. As he finished his sermon, he pled for souls and pressed for decisions in the power of God the Holy Spirit. Surely there was *pathos* in Peter's voice and urgency on his countenance as we read "with many other words he bore witness and continued to exhort them."

Those who extended the gospel appeal in the Bible made it pressing. Paul pressed the claims of Christ to King Agrippa's heart, and the Bible records he almost persuaded him (see Acts 26:28). As pastors seek to draw the net, they need to recapture this spirit of urgency and press for decisions in the power of God's Spirit.

In the preface to this book, we used the illustration of a trial attorney refusing to make a final appeal to the jury to decide in favor of his client. That scenario would be ridiculous and grounds for malpractice for any sane lawyer, yet it happens so often with those advocating the gospel of Jesus Christ. Preachers present the case of Christ, even calling witnesses, and then close their Bibles and walk away when the time comes for them to press for a decision.

Similarly, an effective salesperson knows to "ask for the sale." The salesperson knows the customer has a need and desire for the product—otherwise, the customer would not have come. The salesperson's job is to meet that customer's need by presenting the product and, of course, asking for the sale. For example, a shoe salesperson might ask, *"Would you like to wear these shoes or would you like me to put them in a box for you?"* The minister, therefore, should not neglect asking, *"Would you like to receive the free gift of eternal life right now?"*

EXTENDING THE GOSPEL
INVITATION PRACTICALLY

When given properly and prayerfully, extending an invitation becomes a practical means to an eternally important end. The public appeal can build a bridge for those under the Spirit's convicting power to walk across and receive personal attention. For example, when people respond and stand at the altar, ministers may take that opportunity to take them aside and issue a personal appeal. Thus, the public appeal can be a means of achieving the personal appeal. In addition, the unsaved are often deeply moved when they see a friend or family member respond to the public appeal. Those who respond consequently seem to serve as escorts and encouragers for others to follow.

The pastor should not assume that his hearers know anything about what to do when they are convicted by the Spirit. In virtually every service in a growing church, people are present who have never experienced a public invitation to receive Christ as Savior. Consequently, the pastor needs to spell out in practical terms exactly what he is asking the people to do. For instance:

> *In a moment, I am going to ask you to do something that will take courage. When we bow our hearts in prayer I am going to ask you to stand, leave your seat, and make your way into the aisle. Those next to you will make way for you and will pat you on the back as you go and say, "God bless you."*
>
> *I am going to ask you to make your way down this aisle and stand with me here at the front. You do not have to worry about what to say. I know why you are coming. And by coming, you will be saying, "I am going to go God's way." I will meet you here. Many are going to come, and when we all get here I am going to lead in a prayer. After the prayer we want to invite you into the welcome center and give you some Bible study material that will help you. If you come as an inquirer, we will lead you to faith in Christ Jesus. Remember, you do not need to worry about what to say. By your coming you will be saying that you are going God's way.*

Pastors can seek to be as practical as possible at the time of invitation by putting themselves in a man or woman's place in the pew. He or she has a desire to respond, but does not know what to expect. The pastor communicates exactly what to expect—no surprises—by walking through the steps. Thus, individuals coming forward can know they are not going to have to say anything to the congregation. They can know that the pastor is going to lead the prayer, and they will not be embarrassed.

Making gospel invitations practical also includes adapting the vernacular a preacher uses. Jesus talked about the necessity of continually changing wineskins so the wine might be preserved. Old wineskins lose their elasticity and become brittle. When new wine, still fermenting and expanding its gases, was poured into old wineskins, the wineskins often burst, and both the wine and skin were lost. However, when new wine was poured into new skins, both were preserved (cf. Mark 2:22).

The wine is the gospel message. It never changes. The wineskins are the methods. They constantly change. For example, the vocabulary used in the church is foreign to those in the marketplace. Out of habit, Christians may try to reach a modern, unchurched world with seventeenth-century English—but the lost person does not speak in that manner. He does not ask his secretary, "Wilt thou transcribe this Epistle?" No. He says it like the newer translation, "Will you take a letter?" If pastors do not change their clichés, the world will never respond.

Pastors would do well to choose their words carefully in both public and personal appeals. Avoiding clichés and loaded terms can disarm hearers and convey a sense of warmth and welcome, building a bridge instead of a barrier (for example, using "welcome center" in place of "counseling room"). In addition to being passionate and pious, and personal and persuasive, the pastor should take note of these practical considerations when he extends the gospel appeal.

EXTENDING THE GOSPEL INVITATION PERTINENTLY

The appeal should flow from the body of the gospel presentation and relate to the content of the message. Sadly, many of those extending the appeal have difficulty making a smooth transition into the invitation to receive Christ. Sudden and abrupt transitions from the presentation to the appeal distract the hearer and divert the flow of the speaker. In contrast, during pulpit appeals the invitation should always issue from the thesis of the sermon.

The expository preacher, who teaches verse-by-verse through books of the Bible, may seldom preach what one might refer to as a "hard-core, fire-and-brimstone" evangelistic sermon. However, even these preachers can make strong evangelistic appeals that are pertinent to the message of the exposition itself.

For example, in a sermon from Paul's letter to Philemon, a pastor may be dealing with the subject of interpersonal relationships in the home, the office, and the social arena. When it is time for the appeal, the pastor could transition from information to invitation in the following way:

> There are only three relationships in life. There is an upward expression. That is a relationship with God. This is what makes us different from animals. We have the capacity to connect with God Himself through Jesus Christ. Second, there is the inward expression. We have a relationship with ourselves that involves self-worth, self-respect, and self-love. Finally, there is an outward expression. We have a relationship with others, whether in the home, at school, in the office, or wherever we interact with other people. The truth is, we will never be properly related to others until we are properly related to ourselves. If we have no real self-love or self-respect, we project these into destructive relationships with others. Jesus was on target when He said we should love our neighbor as we love ourselves (cf. Matt 22:39).
>
> However, we must go a step further to find the ultimate truth: we will never be properly related to ourselves unless we are properly related to God by receiving the free gift of eternal life made possible for us through His Son. Only then can we realize how indescribably valuable we are to God and really begin to feel good about ourselves. So, the only way to have positive, profitable interpersonal relationships with others is to have self-worth and self-respect. The only way true self-worth is acquired is in knowing God through the Lord Jesus Christ.

Although the body of a particular message may not be evangelistic in nature, the transition to the evangelistic appeal can be made so that it flows naturally out of the sermon and is pertinent to it.

Moreover, the pastor can make an evangelistic application no matter what the subject of a sermon is. Take, for example, a message on world peace. Jesus has called Christians to be "peacemakers," not just peace lovers. That is, Christians are to promote unity. The transition to the evangelistic appeal might be made like this:

> We will never have peace on a global level until we have peace on a continental level; we will never have peace on a continental level until we have peace on a national level; we will never have peace on a national level until we have peace on a state level; we will never have peace on a state level until we have peace on a county level; we will never have peace on a county level until we have peace on a city level; we will never have peace on a city level until we have peace on a neighborhood level; we will never have peace on a neighborhood level until we have peace on our street; we will never have peace on our street until we have peace on our block; we will never have peace on our block until we have peace in our home; we will never have peace in our home until there is peace in our hearts. And there will never be peace in our hearts until we have made peace with God through our Lord Jesus Christ!

This transition sets the stage for the evangelistic appeal; it is pertinent to the sermon and issues from it. No matter what passage is preached, we can always find a way to make a smooth transition and direct hearers to the cross.

Another method for transitioning could be to use a poem related to the topic. For example, a message on the subject of friendship—what it means to be a true friend—could move into the gospel appeal through the following poem attributed to D. J. Higgins:

> My friend, I stand in judgment now
>   and feel that you're to blame somehow.
> On earth I walked with you day by day
>   and never did you point the way.
> You knew the Lord in truth and glory,
>   but never did you tell the story.
> My knowledge was then very dim,
>   you could have led me safe to Him.
> Though we lived together on the earth,
>   you never told me of the Second Birth.
> And now I stand here condemned,
>   because you failed to mention Him.
> You taught me many things, that's true
>   I called you friend, I trusted you.
> But now I learn that it's too late,
>   you could have saved me from this state.
> We walked and talked, by day, by night;
>   and yet you showed me not the Light.
> You let me live and love and die,
>   you knew I'd never live on high.
> Yes, I called you "friend" in life,
>   and trusted you through joy and strife.
> And yet on coming to the end,
>   now, I cannot call you "my friend."[1]

By utilizing interesting but nonconfrontational content like poetry, the pastor can transition from the body of the sermon on friendship to the evangelistic appeal. Transitions are of vital importance in keeping the attention and interest of hearers, and they should always be pertinent by flowing out of the thesis of the presentation.

EXTENDING THE GOSPEL INVITATION WITH A PLENARY FOCUS

While the personal, private appeal has the profession of faith as its singular focus, the public appeal is plenary in nature. It is all-encompassing. In the corporate worship setting, there are many and varied needs to which the pastor should appeal.

Pastors must seek to fill their congregations' needs week by week. They must be aware that many hearers are in the church out of inquiry or curiosity and have yet to embrace the gospel. There are also those who have accepted Christ during the week as the church members extended a personal appeal to them. These newly saved Christians now need to make their decisions public. There are still others who need to move their church membership.

Finally, many other people do not know what they need to do or how they can respond. The pastor must provide leadership by offering them specific instructions and adopting a plenary approach. It may take five or six minutes to do this at the beginning of a public appeal, but there should be no doubt in the hearers' minds about what they are being asked to do and how they need to respond.

For example, people may be present who need to accept the free gift of eternal life. Pastors could appeal to these individuals in the following manner:

> *I know there are many of you here who have never trusted in Jesus Christ alone for your salvation. If you were to die today, you do not know where you would spend eternity. In just a moment*

I am going to ask you to leave your seat and come and stand with me here at the front. By your coming you will be saying, "I want to know Jesus Christ." Many are going to come, and when we get here, I am going to lead in a prayer. If you are coming as an inquirer, we want to sit down with you and lead you to faith in Jesus Christ.

Those who need to be converted now know what they can do about their condition and what to expect when they respond.

Others in the congregation may have already invited Christ to be their personal Savior, but they need to make a public pledge of their life to Him. Pastors may appeal to this group in the following manner:

There are others of you who have already opened your hearts to Christ, perhaps this week, last week, last month, or whenever, who now need to make public pledges. I am going to ask you to join the others who are coming, and by your coming you will be saying, "I am going to go God's way by openly, unashamedly, and publicly identifying with Him." Jesus said if we would confess Him before people, He would, in turn, confess us before the Father in heaven. There is something about a public decision that will help solidify it in your life. When Christ called people to follow Him, He always did so publicly. It is the right thing to do.

Some in the congregation may be uncertain of their own salvation and need assurance. To these the pastor might add the following:

Many of you are honest enough to say, "I really am unsure about whether I am a Christian." God doesn't want you to wonder and worry from one day to the next whether you are saved or lost. In fact, He says the Bible was written that you may "know that you have eternal life" (1 John 5:13). He says the experience of salvation is like going from death into life or darkness into light. How can you go from a dark room into a light room and not know it? How can you pass from death into life and not know it? God has not made it hard to be saved. In fact, He says that if any of us will come to Him, we must come in simple, childlike faith, trusting in Him alone for salvation.

If you are uncertain, you can settle the matter today. In just a moment I am going to ask you to join the others who are coming. By your coming you will be saying, "I'm not sure I have received eternal life, but I want to be certain, and I want to settle it, once and for all, this morning." I will look for you to be first, and I'll meet you here at the front. We have some material to give you that will help you, and we want to sit down with you and lead you to the assurance of your salvation.

Those hearers who have been wrestling with a lack of assurance now know they are not alone, and they no longer have to be afraid to admit it and to seek guidance.

There may also be yet others in the congregation who are church members and followers of the Lord Jesus Christ but are no longer active in their previous church fellowships. Perhaps they have moved to the area or are attending from other churches for whatever reason. They have a need to unite with the church fellowship here. To these, the pastor may publicly appeal in the following manner:

Many of you are Christians but are no longer active in a local church. This is where you are now eating your spiritual food, and it is now time for you to come out of the shadows and put on the uniform of church membership. You have thought about it, planned on it, prayed about it, and the only thing left is just to

do it. In just a moment I am going to ask you to join the others
who are coming. By your coming you will be saying, "I am going
to put my life in this church and serve God in it and through
it." By your coming you will be an escort for the many who need
to know the Lord Jesus.

Pastors today are ministering in a day when people are not "join-
ers" as they were in the past. So, pastors must use plenary appeals
to encourage this group to lead the way.

When the public appeal is given, it needs to be plenary. Many
lament the fact that more young people are not surrendering to
God's call to the ministry, yet there are thousands of churches
where the appeal to ministry has not been heard from the pulpit
in years. Consequently, pastors must believe in challenging the
people from the pulpit and "calling out the called" through the
public appeal.

EXTENDING THE GOSPEL
INVITATION PERCEPTIVELY

Drawing the net demands a special sensitivity and perceptivity to
the Holy Spirit. There are times in corporate worship when the
pastor may sense a special moving of the Lord on His people,
and the appeal should be offered at that time.

For example, perhaps during a moving solo—before the
sermon—the pastor may recognize God Himself working in
the room. A holy hush may have descended on the congregation.
The pastor, in that moment, should acknowledge God's presence
and give opportunity for a response. He can share the good news
and extend the public appeal right then, and people may respond.

On other occasions, men and women, under the power of
conviction, may leave their seats in the middle of the sermon to

come to the altar. The pastor may need to stop the sermon, offer an appeal, and then continue preaching.

Again, the pastor should be sensitive and perceptive to the leading of the Holy Spirit. Appeals do not have to be given at the same time in the same way as they have always been given.

Pastors should strive to be perceptive—not predictable—regarding the methods they use. In one instance, the pastor could extend the invitation at the conclusion of worship on Sunday morning without any singing. He can ask the congregation to remain seated throughout the appeal. This method removes the perceived inconvenience of trying to exit a pew through people who are standing and singing. Then the pastor can deliver the Sunday morning public appeal and instruct those under conviction to stand, make their way into the aisle, and arrive at the front while the entire congregation prays.

In the quietness of the moment, people will respond. Once they are gathered at the front, the pastor can lead a word of prayer and invite those who responded to go to the welcome center, a space near the auditorium where trained encouragers can deal personally with each person who responded to the gospel. Those joining the church from other congregations should be asked to share their personal salvation testimony with the encourager. It is imperative and important to ensure that those seeking to unite with the church are regenerate.

Occasional services call for a different approach. In a worship experience attracting those who may have been out of church for a long time, such as at Christmas or Easter, the pastor might conclude the message by pointing out an informational card located at each seat. This card could have space for each person's name and address, a place for them to "check" indicating that they would like to know more about spiritual things, and an invitation to visit the welcome center for a reception immediately following the service. The pastor could verbally challenge the hearers to take the card and meet him in this welcome center. Such a place might be a kiosk in the lobby with a sign entitled "First Steps" so that it is easily recognized. This is an adaptation of what the evangelist Charles Finney used to call the "anteroom." Churches may find this to be an effective tool for more contemporary worship.

A midweek worship service may call for another type of approach and appeal. The service could conclude with a call for prayer for the sick. Those who desire prayer could be asked to come and kneel at the appointed place where the elders stand ready to pray. Provide room for those who physically need God's touch as well as for those sick in their souls and spiritual lives (think brokenhearted, depression, etc.).

This holistic prayer approach incorporates the needs of spirit, soul, and body. During this time of gathering and prayer, the pastor may address the rest of the congregation:

> *Many of you know someone who needs prayer at this altar, but they are not here requesting it. Perhaps they cannot be. Maybe they are physically sick and in the hospital. In a moment you will want to come and kneel in their place, as it were, and be an intercessor for them. Perhaps you know someone sick in soul, brokenhearted, depressed, or just emotionally burned out, and they are not here requesting prayer for themselves. In just a moment you will want to come and kneel in their place and intercede on their behalf.*
>
> *Or perhaps you know someone who is sick spiritually or is spiritually dead without Christ. They are not here tonight calling on the Lord to save them, but in a moment you will want to come and kneel in their place and become an intercessor for them.*

The congregation can sing a brief chorus while those people move to the altar. After a prayer, the pastor can then say:

*Now, before we return to our seats I know there are many of you
who would say, "I am not sure I have eternal life, but I'd like to
receive it, and I'd like to settle it tonight." While we continue in
a spirit of prayer, if that is your case, would you just quickly lift
your hand and then put it down?*

The pastor may then transition into inviting those who admit
their need to the welcome center where the ministers can address
them on a personal basis.

Every time a church meets, people should be given an opportunity to respond to the call of Christ. For example, consider a
church that hosts large Bible studies for business people. It could
place registration cards on every table and request attendees to
share their contact information and indicate whether they have
prayed to receive Christ. As the study leader closes in prayer,
he can appeal to the hearers to open their lives to Christ in the
privacy of their own prayers. He might direct them to respond
on the cards if they feel called to do so. The Bible study leader
can then collect the cards and personally follow up with everyone
who responded to give them Bible study materials and instructions on how to act on their decision for Christ.

Some churches are more technologically equipped than
others. They may use modern technology's innovative ways to
reach people with the gospel in and through the public worship
service. These days it is safe to assume that almost everyone
carries a mobile phone device. At the conclusion of the sermon,
the pastor might lead into the gospel invitation by inviting those
under his hearing to pray the sinner's prayer with him. He can
call upon them to "confess" this decision by typing the word
"DECIDED" into a text number such as "777777." The church
can then be prepared with a series of five-minute videos on new
life in Christ, which it could send to the new believer over a series
of days following his or her decision. These videos would include

what it means to trust in Christ, how to begin to read the Bible, how to pray, and several "next steps" in the believer's walk with Christ, while helping to connect him or her with the ministries of the local church. This same process can be simultaneously provided for someone who may be watching the service online through a live video stream. The minister can also direct him or her to use the direct message feature of the social media medium which the service is being broadcast through.

Another innovative way to encourage listeners to respond to the gospel is by using a QR code. A QR code could be attached to the backs of the pews or theater seats, or it can be projected on a screen. At the time of invitation the pastor can invite inquirers to open the camera app of their mobile phones and point their camera lenses toward the code, which would provide them with links to record their decisions, along with information about the next steps of their Christian discipleship.

Innovation does not always require technology or something new. Recall in the Gospels the many times Jesus had meals with people, whether at the home of Matthew in Capernaum, Mary and Martha in Bethany, or Simon the Pharisee. One effective way of offering the gospel invitation is when pastors host quarterly dinners. The pastor can invite all the people who have visited church in the past three months. In cases where there are a lot of attendees, hosts can be placed at each table to make everyone feel welcomed. During the dinner, the pastor makes his way around the tables and personally visits all the guests. Then he shares the gospel with them in that setting and gives them an opportunity then and there to trust in Christ and even join the fellowship of the church.

Some pastors also offer more of a "go out" invitation in place of the "come forward" invitation. In other words, at the end of the service the pastor may lead his hearers to faith in Christ and ask them to take a card from the pew/chair rack, complete the information, and "go out" to a welcome center or kiosk in the lobby. When they arrive to the designated location, they can exchange the card for a Bible and helpful materials to grow in Christ.

The perceptive pastor may seek to build spiritual confidence in those about to respond to the invitation. Rather than asking people to stand immediately, the pastor may invite the congregation at the conclusion of the message to bow their heads in prayer. Then he shares a brief gospel presentation, asks people to raise their hands if they would like to receive Christ, and encourages them to look up at him and stand where they are to invite Christ into their lives. Then the pastor might invite them to meet him at a designated place after the service to provide them with some materials to help in their new walk with Christ.

Preachers need to learn an indefinite number of methods to offer the gospel to their audiences. These methods require them to be perceptive of their audiences and the Holy Spirit. In short, there is no need to be continually repetitive and predictable in the gospel approach. Churches do not always have to sing four verses of *Just as I Am* and pressure people through all sorts of manipulation into a response. Regular church attenders will be prone to lose their sense of expectancy if preachers fall into a routine that never changes, and newcomers will wonder what they should do. Many pastors assume that the ones who really need to respond understand the invitation process, but this assumption will produce Sunday invitations that have little visible response.

EXTENDING THE GOSPEL INVITATION PROVOCATIVELY

Nothing Christians do should be more alluring, more captivating, more inviting, or more provocative than appealing to individuals to become followers of the Lord Jesus Christ. Pastors have many avenues to break out of established patterns so their personal and public appeals can capture the attention of their hearers, arouse their curiosity, and increase their appetites to know more about Christ so they can receive Him in faith.

The life of the Lord shows that He had an ability not only to analyze people's concerns but also to arouse their curiosity. Consider, for example, His encounter with the woman at the well in John 4. Simply by talking with her, He demolished social, religious, racial, and political barriers that existed in first-century Middle Eastern culture. He aroused her curiosity by speaking to her about "living water" so that she asked, "Sir, . . . where do you get that living water?" (v. 11). His provocative approach moved her to question Him—and that questioning technique is an important factor to consider when issuing public appeals.

Preachers cannot create a spiritual interest in a person. Only the Holy Spirit can generate such an interest, for no one has ever truly come to Jesus Christ who was not first drawn by the Father (cf. 6:44). But Christians can be His instruments to arouse curiosity and share Jesus Christ in the power of the Spirit while leaving the results to God. It is important to remember that when God is working, He is working on both ends of the spectrum. If He leads a Philip to the Gaza desert, He will have an Ethiopian there ready to hear and receive the good news. If He leads a Peter to Caesarea, He will have a Cornelius there ready to hear and receive the good news. If He leads our Lord to go out of His way and through Samaria to a well, He will have a woman there ready to hear and receive the good news. If He leads a Christian to some particular place at some particular time, He is desiring that this Christian be His hand extended in passing the cup of living water.

Since pastors are particularly called to offer the public appeal with regularity, they should seek to arouse the curiosity of the congregation at different times during the course of the worship service as they pray toward and plan for the time of invitation. Early in the service, when they welcome guests, pastors may say something like, *"Some of you have come here unaware that this will be the supreme hour of your life, for this morning you are going to make life's most important discovery and leave here in a few minutes with a brand-new life and a new beginning!"* This type of statement arouses the curiosity of those who hear it and gives them something to think about as they hear the music and listen to the message. Pastors can then tie that statement back into their public appeals.

Presenting the gospel in an appealing and provocative manner could be the approach needed to persuade people to respond.

EXTENDING THE GOSPEL INVITATION PERVASIVELY

The public appeal has been a regular fixture in many evangelical churches for so long that it can unfortunately become compartmentalized and robotically administered, with little expectancy and anticipation, at a set time following the sermon and preceding the benediction. The public appeal must become more of an attitude than a mere activity in worship. Awareness of the appeal should permeate the entire worship experience from beginning to end. This attitude should begin before the service, continue throughout the service, extend after the message, and linger in people's minds even after their dismissal. The public appeal should thus be, in one word, *pervasive*.

In the valuable time before the service, the pastor should walk the aisles of the auditorium, greeting the very people to whom he will make the appeal later in the service. This is a splendid opportunity to speak to scores of people, shake their hands, and touch their lives. Church members may wave the pastor over to introduce him to friends they had led to Christ during the week, giving him the chance to know who they are and rejoice with them in their newfound faith.

In these preservice meetings with new Christians, the pastor might tell them the following:

> *At the end of my message this morning, I am going to ask all those who have received Christ this week to leave their seats and join me for a prayer at the front, and I am going to look for you to be the first one to come! Our mutual friend Bob, here, will come with you, and you can stand together for Christ.*

Thus, people can commit to make a public pledge during the invitation before the service even begins. These preservice appeals can have a disarming effect on those who have the deepest need to respond to the appeal. It gives them an opportunity to affirm their faith to the minister and removes the mystery of why they are coming forward during the invitation.

As the service begins, the worship experience may include a time to be still and acknowledge the presence of the living Lord in the midst of the church. During this prayer time, the pastor could extend the appeal by inviting the congregation to pray for those in the service who find themselves at some intersection of life with little purpose and perhaps no direction. People in the congregation should thank God in advance for the many who might respond to the passionate appeal later in the service. This prayer can include words for those on each person's right and left so that everyone in the building may be brought before the Lord at the point of their need. The appeal may continue by welcoming guests with the positive affirmation: *"Many of you have come thinking you are merely attending a worship service, but you are here this morning to keep a divine appointment with God Himself, and you will leave here in a few minutes with a brand-new life and a brand-new beginning!"* This time of prayer can turn on a light in the minds of people, causing them to anticipate and give serious consideration to the claims of Christ.

The pastor may seek to build hope and expectancy in the hearts of hearers as he continues to issue the appeal in various ways throughout the service. For example, the introduction to the sermon can provide a "hook" for the appeal, and this theme can recur throughout the message. The pastor also should plan for a smooth transition from the sermon into the formal public appeal during his time of study. All of this preparation, along with intentional appeals throughout the service, should lead into the crucial moment when the pastor invites a response to the gospel of Jesus Christ. This moment thus becomes the hinge on which the experience of corporate worship turns.

Even after the time of invitation has concluded, appeals should continue. As ministers and counselors meet with those who gathered at the altar, the pastor may once again address the congregation:

I know that many of you have never been in a service like this one, and you may feel in your heart that you should have responded with these others to Christ's appeal this morning. However, it is not unusual in our church for people to continue to come even during the offering. Our ministers will be at the end of your aisle here at the front to receive you. By your coming forward during the offering, you will be saying that you do not want to leave here this morning without settling with Christ. Don't go away without Him. Come now even during the offering, and take one of the ministers by the hand; they know why you are coming.

In this example the church collects the offering *after* the sermon, allowing the spirit of the appeal to be carried over during the playing of the offertory.

As the pastor dismisses the people, he may be aware that many of his hearers are under the conviction of the Holy Spirit and are about to leave without making a conscious decision for Christ. Perhaps he could give people another way to respond by directing them to fill out an information card, encouraging them to take that card to the welcome center if they are interested in knowing more about spiritual things. That card could be one more path to a gospel conversation.

Finally, the pastor should challenge the congregation to be about the business of extending the personal appeal throughout the week: *"Someone you know needs to receive Jesus this week. I will be looking for you and that someone by your side next Sunday!"* The public appeal thus should not be thought of as a single, solitary portion of the corporate worship experience; it is an attitude that must permeate the entire life of the congregation.

EXTENDING THE GOSPEL
INVITATION PRECLUSIVELY

One of the most important factors to be considered by those who extend the appeal is to preclude certain fears and objections that weigh on the minds of hearers. Pastors should take time to consider the unspoken barriers and preconceived ideas which hearers feel might keep them from Christ. The best means of helping people change their minds (repent) and answer their objections is with the Word of God.

Some hearers do not respond to the appeal for receiving Christ because everything is so new to them and they are afraid of what others might think. To be sensitive to this objection, the pastor may say the following:

> *I know that some of you are wondering what others might think of you if you join those who have come to respond openly and publicly to Christ's call. However, I want to remind you that Jesus said, "Whoever is ashamed of me and of my words . . . of him will the Son of Man also be ashamed when he comes in the glory of his Father" (Mark 8:38). Be more concerned this morning about what Christ will think than what others will think.*

By using God's Word in the time of appeal, the pastor, with great authority, can break down a barrier and build a bridge over a difficult objection, making it easier for hearers to come to Christ.

Others in the "valley of decision" may fear that because of a previous problematic lifestyle God will not accept them. The pastor should not preclude this objection with shortsighted human wisdom, but always with the Word of God:

> *I sense that some of you are afraid to be vulnerable, worrying that if you respond to Christ He may not accept you. Well, I have good news for you. Jesus said, "Whoever comes to me I will never cast out" (John 6:37). He will receive you just as you are and make something beautiful out of your life.*

In times of appeal, God's Word is the most effective weapon. For example, some individuals fail to respond to the gospel because they have known and watched Christians who were inconsistent. Pastors can appeal to those questioners by reminding them that "[everyone must] give an account of himself to God" (Rom 14:12). Other hearers may be unwilling to give up all to follow the Lord Jesus. They need to be reminded of His piercing question: "For what does it profit a man to gain the whole world and forfeit his soul" (Mark 8:36)? Another group of hearers see no real need to respond to Christ because they feel they are doing the best they can and think God should accept that. This group should be warned that the Bible says, "For whoever keeps the whole law but fails in one point has become guilty of all of it" (Jas 2:10). Some individuals genuinely feel that they have sinned too much to come forward; pastors can break down their barriers with the beautiful fact that "though your sins are like scarlet, they shall be as white as snow" (Isa 1:18). Finally, one of the most perplexing dangers for hearers is when they think that they will have adequate time in the future to respond to Christ's call even if they postpone coming forward now. It behooves pastors to remind them that the Bible says, "Do not boast about tomorrow, for you do not know what a day may bring" (Prov 27:1). The simple truth is, there will not always be adequate time to respond in faith.

The time of public and personal appeal is when the fiercest spiritual battles are being waged. The enemy seeks to put all kinds of objections and fears in the minds of the hearers. The only valid offensive weapon in this conflict is the Word of God, which must be used to make the appeal preclusive.

EXTENDING THE GOSPEL
INVITATION PRUDENTLY

The issuance of Christ's appeal demands truth and honor on the part of the person who extends it. Some pastors and evangelists have lost credibility with their congregations by not being prudent in the pulpit. For example, the speaker can do serious damage to the integrity of the appeal in offhanded statements.

He may say, *"We will sing two more stanzas of invitation, and if no one comes forward we will close the appeal"*—but then after these two stanzas he continues pressing the congregation. This seemingly superficial dishonesty can have a grave impact.

Above all else, the public appeal demands prudence from the one called to extend it. The same is true for those engaged in presenting the personal and private appeal to others. Christians can exercise prudence by being honest, open, and truthful in their approach. The reputation of the Lord is at stake as people witness of Him and offer His appeal.

Honesty in Christ's appeal means the speaker has adequately presented the gospel before offering it to others. While an evangelistic appeal should be given after the gospel is presented, the speaker must remember that the *gospel* should always be presented before an appeal is offered. Some evangelists tell one deathbed story after another, moving on the emotions of the hearers. Yet they never zero in on the good news: "For our sake he made him to be sin who knew no sin, so that in him we might become the righteousness of God" (2 Cor 5:21). Strictly emotional appeals, devoid of the heart of the gospel, may be a reason why many new converts fall away.

There is certainly nothing wrong with having an emotional element in the appeal. After all, Jesus called His hearers in Jerusalem to repentance by passionately comparing Himself to a mother hen gathering her chicks under her wings (Matt 23:37–39). But it is wrong and dishonest for Christians to offer an appeal that is devoid of the heart of the gospel and is not clear about the demands of discipleship.

Hearers may be forgiving, but they will have a hard time overlooking dishonesty, manipulation, and trickery from a Christian. Believers should be truthful in their appeals because they stand as Christ's representative to a lost world. They cannot give people a false hope, but rather prudently need to extend the appeal to people desperately in need of the purpose and peace that only Christ can give.

CONCLUSION

Articulating gospel invitations throughout your sermon, as well as its conclusion, is not a matter of memorizing the templates provided in this chapter. Instead, these examples provide you with a model of how to verbalize the spiritual needs and/or problems within the passage of Scripture you preach in such a way that you anticipate the questions your listeners have and/or the decisions they may consider making after hearing your message. Additionally, some of the samples intend to remind you that unbelievers may be unfamiliar with the specific ways and venues that your church has established to provide consultation, assistance, and answers to those interested in making a spiritual decision. For this reason, you must be precise in your explanations of how, when, and where those who want to receive the gospel or gain more information about it can do so.

BEST PRACTICES IN ISSUING PUBLIC GOSPEL INVITATIONS

THIS BOOK HAS PRESENTED EVIDENCE THAT PUBLIC INVITA-
tions are replete throughout the Bible. In addition to this biblical
precedent, other supplementary reasons were offered to support
the use of invitations for today. Suggestions for preparing and
delivering public appeals for unbelievers to repent and believe
were then given. The book now concludes by integrating its
featured precepts with practical applications in order to recom-
mend some best practices of (1) issuing public gospel invitations
and (2) assisting new disciples to assimilate into the local church
and progress in Christian maturity.

MAKE YOUR GOSPEL INVITATIONS PROPHETIC

From where do preachers receive their authority when they
speak before crowds of people and offer Christ's appeal for men
and women to receive the free gift of eternal life? What is the
source of their authority when they stand behind pulpits and

appeal to their hearers to accept Christ as their personal Savior? Those who make a public appeal for sinners to trust Christ do so as God's spokesmen and representatives, with all the authority of heaven. So when preachers offer Christ's appeal, they should make sure it is *prophetic*—that is, authoritative and biblically based.

When Simon Peter stood before the multitude on the day of Pentecost, he invoked Joel 2:28–32 and established a prophetic, biblical basis for (1) what was happening and (2) what he desired his hearers to do in response. He continued to interject the Scriptures (Pss 16; 110) throughout his message, and his appeal had the authority of heaven because it was prophetic and biblical. Consequently, any congregation should be alarmed when its preacher fails to include and leverage the Word of God in his gospel appeals. A preacher who offers an appeal to receive Christ without being prophetic—that is, not bringing the Word of God to bear on a specific occasion—would be like a surgeon who goes into surgery without a scalpel. On the contrary, the Word of God "cuts to the heart" when it is used, as evidenced in Peter's Pentecostal proclamation (Acts 2:37) and the testimony of the author of Hebrews (Heb 4:12).

Those who enjoy the greatest harvest in their public and personal appeals for others to follow Christ share a common characteristic. They are *prophetic*—that is, they strongly proclaim the Word of God in their approaches. For example, a commitment to use the Bible in public gospel invitations was a basic clue to the success of Billy Graham's public ministry. His proclamation was punctuated with the phrase, "The Bible says . . ." perhaps dozens of times in any of his messages and appeals.

Being prophetic in an appeal is *profitable*. The apostle Paul wrote to his young understudy Timothy to remind him, "All

Scripture is breathed out by God and profitable for teaching, for reproof, for correction, and for training in righteousness, that the man of God may be complete, equipped for every good work" (2 Tim 3:16–17). An effective appeal is a balanced appeal—that is, it is doctrinally sound, reproves, gently corrects, and instructs in righteousness. Unfortunately, a number of those who preach the gospel see little fruit because their appeals are out of balance, overemphasizing one particular element. Not a few people issue appeals full of doctrine to the exclusion of instruction. Some excessively rebuke, turning people away. Still others think every appeal must be used to correct everyone else.

As the first chapter of this book demonstrated, the Bible illustrates prophetic, authoritative appeals all the way from Genesis to Revelation. For example, in Genesis 3:9 God initiated a conversation with Adam in order to restore their broken fellowship. He called out to Adam, "Where are you?" God knew where Adam was hiding, but He wanted Adam to acknowledge where he was and why he was there. Next, Joshua, with heaven's authority behind him, declared to the Israelites in Canaan, "Choose this day whom you will serve. . . . But as for me and my house, we will serve the LORD" (Josh 24:15). Later on, Elijah exclaimed to the people of Israel on Mount Carmel, "How long will you go limping between two different opinions? If the LORD is God, follow him; but if Baal, then follow him" (1 Kgs 18:21). Finally, on the last page of the Bible both the Holy Spirit and the Church prophetically issue the following appeal: "'Come.' . . . And let the one who is thirsty come; let the one who desires take the water of life without price" (Rev 22:17). Thus, the Bible, from cover to cover, serves as the source of prophetic authority. For this reason, when preachers proclaim the gospel, they should do so with heaven's authority behind them.

MAKE YOUR GOSPEL
INVITATIONS PENETRATING

Peter's Pentecostal appeal had a penetrating effect on his hearers. Their hearts were "cut," which led them to ask, "What shall we do?" (Acts 2:37). In the Christian vocabulary, *cut* described the Holy Spirit's *convicting* them. In contrast, many modern appeals are superficial or are designed to make the hearers feel good. Some churches even rejoice in the fact that they encourage people to attend without making them feel guilty about their lifestyles, whatever these may be. Simon Peter's appeal did not have that effect; it cut and pierced his hearers to the heart. Peter's direct appeal, in the power of the Holy Spirit, is the reason three thousand were saved and baptized that day. Perhaps today's ambiguous appeals are the reason churches in the Southern Baptist Convention, today's greatest missionary-sending denomination, only average baptizing three people in an entire year!

A person will consider the cross a farce unless he recognizes that he cannot satisfy the righteous demands of God's law. However, when his heart is cut—when conviction of sin becomes a personal matter—this person becomes aware that his only hope of being right with God is through the cross of Christ. Countless people in many church services have never felt conviction because they have never heard appeals that were prophetic, plain, positive, and personal.

A pastor can be contemporary in his approach to grow his church while still insisting that his hearers grasp what Peter's hearers realized—their own personal responsibility for the death of Jesus Christ. When the men and women at Pentecost realized what they had done in crucifying the Lord, their hearts were broken (Acts 2:23–37). In attempting to draw the net today, too few pastors attempt to lead their hearers to assume personal responsibility for their sins. Consequently, many appeals are not penetrating and leave their hearers without conviction, resulting in few conversions.

Conviction always precedes conversion. This process is referred to as *spiritual birth* (e.g., John 3:1–10; Titus 3:5; 1 Pet 1:23). Consider its relationship to physical birth. Pain precedes the birth of a child, and the same is true with spiritual birth: godly sorrow over sin is necessary for supernatural, new birth. Many empty churches have lists of inactive members who merely "made a decision" early in life, knowing nothing of conviction and conversion.

Good farmers know they will never reap a bountiful crop until they prepare and plant it. First, they mount their tractors and plow their fields in order to break and bust up the sod. Then they plant the seed and cultivate, water, and nurture the crop. The harvest consequently arrives, and the farmers glean it.

Pastors may make appeals for Christ and wonder why they seldom experience a harvest. Perhaps the ground has not been broken? The Word of God, like a sharp, two-edged sword, is the only tool that can cut to the heart. Appeals for Christ thus need to penetrate and break the ground of the heart. No matter how much seed is sown or how much time is spent in nurturing, the harvest will not come if the ground is not broken.

MAKE YOUR GOSPEL INVITATIONS PERSUASIVE

The practice of God-anointed appeals involves persuasion. Preachers should be so straightforward and persuasive in issuing their gospel invitations that their hearers should begin wondering how to respond to the profound need they are feeling in their hearts: "What am I being asked to do, and how do I do it?" Those who find themselves under the Holy Spirit's conviction of sin ask these questions because they do not know what to do when they hear the gospel preached and experience this conviction. They cannot comprehend how they can and should respond to the call to become Jesus's disciple because they lack spiritual discernment (cf. 1 Cor 2:14).

Many of the gospel appeals issued today fall on deaf ears because they lack direct and precise clarity. Instead of being clear, they sound complicated. In place of being positive, they come across as critical. Unduly blunt forthrightness is substituted for ambiguity. No wonder men and women ask themselves when they hear the gospel, "What must I do?"

The ways by which unbelievers are persuaded vary from person to person. Our Lord's earliest followers, for example, differed in how they were persuaded to follow Him. John and Andrew were persuaded to follow Christ through the means of *public proclamation*. They joined the throngs of people who flocked to the Jordan Valley to hear John the Baptist preach repentance. He attempted to persuade his hearers through direct means by declaring, "Behold, the Lamb of God, who takes away the sin of the world!" (John 1:29). Upon hearing this public proclamation, John and Andrew "followed Jesus" (v. 37).

Simon Peter and Nathanael, on the other hand, were persuaded to follow the Lord through *personal conversation*—Peter through his family and Nathanael by means of his friend. Having found Christ through *public proclamation*, Andrew's first impulse led him to confront his brother, Peter, claiming that Jesus was the Messiah. He sought, taught, and then brought Peter to Jesus (cf. vv. 41–42). Philip did the same; however, his appeal was directed toward his friend instead of his family. He went to Nathanael, pressed the claims of Christ to his heart, and then simply and persuasively challenged him, "Come and see" (vv. 45–51).

Pastors and preachers will never draw the net and win the world only through their *public proclamation*. They are also obligated to appeal to others persuasively by way of their *personal conversations*. Andrew found Peter. Jesus found Philip. And Philip found Nathanael.

The kingdom of God has continued to grow through the centuries by its adherents personally confronting unbelievers with the gospel. The most far-reaching results were achieved in that first generation without the forums, technology, and media available to Christians in the twenty-first century. The good news spread from lip to ear until it reached all the way to Rome itself. Within the first one hundred years of Christianity, paganism was shaken to its center by a one-on-one, persuasive, personal confrontation which began when "[Andrew] first found his own brother Simon and said to him, 'We have found the Messiah' (which means Christ). He brought him to Jesus" (vv. 41–42).

Although they were all persuaded in different ways, these early followers of Christ were essentially brought to the same question—"What shall we do?" The Baptizer's *public proclamation* persuaded John and Andrew, but Peter and Nathanael were persuaded by Andrew and Philip's *personal conversation*. Thus, Christians should be persuasive in making Christ's appeal, whether publicly from pulpits or personally through conversations.

Personal gospel conversations on Mondays through Saturdays will influence and impact public gospel proclamations on Sundays. First, a preacher who converses with unbelievers during the week will find those same people more likely to hear him on the weekends because he personally took time to interact with them. Second, these conversations will teach him more about the kind of people to whom he will preach each week. And, finally, the Lord tends to bless the public preaching of a preacher who personally shares the gospel.

MAKE YOUR GOSPEL
INVITATIONS POINTED

Repentance is a forgotten word in Christian vocabulary today, primarily because many Christians are confused about what it really is and how to put it into action. They often confuse repentance in appeals with *remorse*—but merely being sorry for sin is not repentance. For example, the rich young ruler was "sorrowful" (Matt 19:22), but he did not accept Christ's appeal and walked away instead. Christians also confuse repentance with *regret*—but simply wishing something had not happened is not repentance. After all, Pilate washed his hands in regret over his deed, but he had rejected Jesus Christ by having him executed. Still other Christians confuse repentance with *resolve*—but simply determining to take on a new set of moral standards and "turn over a new leaf" is not repentance.

Until repentance is clearly defined, a pastor's appeal will never be properly pointed. Repentance stems from a Greek word (*metanoeo*), which means "a change of mind." When one repents, one changes one's mind about four basic things.

First, repentance results in a change of mind about *self*. Upon repentance, a person has a new attitude about his sense of self-importance—he now puts God above himself. Repentance is also a change of mind about *sin*. A repentant person no longer sees his sin as an inconsequential vice to laugh off, excuse, or minimize, instead sensing that this sin is serious enough to put the Lord on the cross. Repentance is also a change of mind about the *Savior*. A repentant person perceives Him to be not only a great teacher or leader but the promised Messiah, God Himself who came to save the world. Finally, repentance causes a change of mind about *salvation*, which is understood not to be an award that can be earned or deserved but God's gracious gift to all who will receive it.

A pastor does not have to use the word *repent* when he appeals to unbelievers that they should follow Christ, but he must at least convey the concept to them. Those who hear such an appeal and actually repent will begin to love what they used to hate and hate what they used to love. Pastors can reject a "turn-or-burn" approach and call people to repent in a positive manner by modeling their approach on Paul's, who wrote that "God's kindness is meant to lead you to repentance" (Rom 2:4). The word picture depicts a gentle father who takes his child by the hand and leads him.

This pointed approach to the call to repent as a part of the gospel appeal is followed by every New Testament preacher. Consider John the Baptist. He appealed to his hearers to "Repent, for the kingdom of heaven is at hand" (Matt 3:2). He spoke without fear or favor—and thousands came to hear him.

The Lord Jesus Himself also followed the same approach, commencing His ministry with an appeal to repent. The Bible says, "From that time Jesus began to preach, saying, 'Repent, for the kingdom of heaven is at hand'" (Matt 4:17). He continued to reassert this appeal in His preaching: "Unless you repent, you will all likewise perish" (Luke 13:3). Even through the conclusion of His work on earth, Jesus reiterated this same message, reminding His followers just before His ascension that "repentance for the forgiveness of sins should be proclaimed in his name to all nations" (24:47). The apostles continued to make this pointed appeal: "Repent therefore, and turn back, that your sins may be blotted out" (Acts 3:19). Repentance from sins was the message of both Peter and Paul, and it must be the message of anyone, anywhere, who urges others to become followers of the Lord Jesus.

General appeals are problematic because they lack a call to decisive action. Many people, especially after public appeals, have no clue what the speaker has challenged them to do.

However, when Christians publicly or privately present the gospel to men and women, they need to urge them to decide, to choose. After all, believers are calling on their hearers to change their minds and receive from God the gracious gift of salvation which Christians hold dearly to their own hearts. This demands a pointed approach. Unfortunately, certain knowledgeable and educated pastor-teachers today seem to be arguing in favor of a salvation that is devoid of any repentance and discipleship, much less any evidence that one has passed from "death into life." Nevertheless, Christians must be absolutely pointed and plain about what the gospel is as we navigate our current days of confusion about the basic tenets of the faith.

Over one hundred years ago, Charles Haddon (C. H.) Spurgeon of England preached, "I cannot conceive it possible for anyone to truly receive Christ as Savior and yet not to receive Him as Lord. . . . A man who is really saved by Grace does not need to be told that He [*sic*] is under solemn obligations to serve Christ—the new life within him tells him that."[1] This is the good news. The most pointed question in all the Bible was asked by the jailer in Philippi. Having come under the conviction of the Holy Spirit, he asked Paul and Silas, "Sirs, what must I do to be saved?" And their pointed reply? "Believe in the Lord Jesus, and you will be saved" (Acts 16:30–31).

Jesus is Lord and anyone who comes to Him does so in true repentance and faith. Repentance and faith are two sides of the same coin, and they are both "not of works" but the gift of God's grace which He grants to unbelievers. This truth should be preachers' pointed appeal. They are partners with God in appealing to others to receive His wonderful gift, but it is God alone who convicts of sin, draws the sinner to Himself, and grants the gift of repentance and faith. Preachers are consequently responsible to make it clear to their hearers that they are coming to Christ and not merely to "the front of the church."

MAKE YOUR GOSPEL
INVITATIONS PIOUS

Christians extending Christ's appeal should be cautious to remember that salvation is the work of God from start to finish: "Salvation belongs to the LORD!" (Jonah 2:9). Only the Holy Spirit can convince people that they have a deep need to change their minds and receive Christ. The Spirit can be grieved and quenched by those who seek to berate, manipulate, maneuver, scold, or cajole their hearers into a "decision."

Appealing "piously" refers to "fearing" the Lord (living in reverential awe of Him), recognizing His sovereignty, and totally depending on Him to do His work of conviction and conversion. He is the One who "adds to the church." He has not called pastors to be responsible for the results but to be consistent and faithful in their witness by life and lip.

God calls people in two ways—through an outward call and an inward call. Simon Peter at Pentecost was keenly aware of this fact. He gave the outward call, but not all of his hearers were saved that day. In fact, some "mocked" him. The three thousand converted to Christ were those who heard not only the outward call but also an inward call. The ones genuinely saved that day, and in this day, are those "whom the Lord our God calls to himself" (Acts 2:39). This is where piety must accompany the appeal. The Christian's assignment is to extend the outward call and trust in the Holy Spirit to issue the inward call.

How can two people sit in the same pew in the same worship service, sing the same songs, hear the same sermon proclaimed in the same anointing of the Holy Spirit, and yet have diametrically opposed responses? One person walks out of the service with no inclination to respond and sees absolutely no need to accept Christ. In contrast, the other person sitting on the same pew falls under conviction of sin and openly responds to the gospel appeal. How does this happen? They both heard the outward call, but only one sensed the inward call. We see the answer in the apostle Paul's ministry. As Paul was extending the appeal by the riverside in Philippi, the Bible records, "One who heard us was a woman named Lydia, from the city of Thyatira, a seller of purple goods, who was a worshiper of God. *The Lord opened her heart* to pay attention to what was said by Paul" (16:14, emphasis added). Paul issued the outward call, and the Lord spoke to Lydia's heart, issuing the inward call.

A few extremists have overemphasized the inward call to the point of perverting the Scriptures and denying the free offer of good news. On the contrary, a pious approach, acknowledging that salvation is God's work, should not diminish a Christian's intensity in issuing the appeal and sharing the glorious gospel with every last person on the planet. In fact, Christians should gain confidence and boldness from the awareness that they are participating with the Father Himself in this miraculous work of salvation.

The pastor's key task is to extend the outward call and trust God to do the work of issuing the inward call by opening the hearers' hearts. It is a privilege to be Christ's extended hand in any situation, whether standing behind a pulpit, sitting in a locker room, visiting around the coffee table, or sitting next to someone on an airplane seat. Jesus affirms this in two statements: "As the Father has sent me, even so I am sending you" (John 20:21) and "For the Son of Man came to seek and to save the lost" (Luke 19:10). Ministers of the gospel of Jesus Christ cannot save men and women, but they can seek them and extend the outward call, leaving the results to Him; for only the Holy Spirit can offer the inward call.

In the words of an old hymn, "Brethren, We Have Met to Worship," "All is vain unless the Spirit of the Holy One comes down." Be sensitive in extending the appeal. As we noted in the beginning of this section, Christians should not try to do the work of the Holy Spirit. He is often grieved and quenched by manipulation and man-centered methods.

The last invitation of the Bible beckons, "The Spirit and the Bride say, 'Come.' . . . And let the one who is thirsty come; let the one who desires take the water of life without price" (Rev 22:17). The Bible states the call of the gospel plainly, left for all posterity. The Bride, the church of the Lord Jesus Christ, calls, "Come!" This is the outward call. The Spirit summons, "Come!" This is the inward call. Both calls are essential and pivotal in "drawing the net" and reaching the world for Christ.

MAKE YOUR GOSPEL INVITATIONS PASSIONATE

If preachers press for decisions with fleshly means and motives, the result will be nothing but "a noisy gong or a clanging cymbal" (1 Cor 13:1). However, when the appeal is pressed out of the passion of a heart burning for God, it will produce lasting results.

Some who preach the Word may become too "professional" in their approaches. This generation's ministry is blessed with digital devices, online Christian bookstores, podcasts, preaching conferences, and around-the-clock Christian television and radio. Today's preachers are in danger of focusing more on their personal branding and polished products than on exhibiting a passion that only comes from being alone with God in His Word.

It is sheer hypocrisy for someone to offer a public invitation who seldom or never privately invites men and women to receive Christ in the normal traffic patterns of life. Discerning individuals can usually listen to a preacher issue a public appeal and tell in an instant whether that person is a soul-winner. Evidence to the contrary normally shows in the passion of his voice and countenance—an untrue ring or a lack of fervor. If a preacher is not personally issuing the appeal day by day, it is difficult for that same person to be passionate when he issues the appeal in the pulpit.

All Christ's followers, especially those who are called into vocational gospel ministry, should be active in personally sharing their faith. In 2021, it took eighty-eight Southern Baptists, with their over forty-seven thousand churches and over thirteen million members, to baptize one person. In fifty-two weeks of public appeals, ten thousand pastors do not make disciples through their public preaching ministries, nor do they train their members to do so. Why? Sadly, there is often little passion in the pulpit. Real passion issues from a lifestyle that personally shares Christ with others and presses for a decision in the power of the Holy Spirit—a burning heart spilling over onto others around it. Passion in public proclamation flows out from passion in personal and private proclamation in the home, the office, an airplane, or the social arena.

W. Fred Swank served as pastor of the Sagamore Hill Baptist Church in Fort Worth, Texas, for forty-three years. He never stood on Sunday morning to offer a public appeal without making sure that he had offered personal and private appeals during the week. "I can tell you if a man is personally and privately sharing his faith by the passion he displays when he does so publicly on Sunday morning from the pulpit," explained Swank. Saturday was a workday for Swank, since he would visit three or four homes to witness for Christ. No wonder he was so effective in his invitations on Sundays; they were the natural overflow of a soul-winner's heart. Swank had personally won many of the men and women who comprised the church leadership to Christ in their homes, and as a result the Sagamore Hill church was an evangelistic pacesetter and annually baptized hundreds of new converts over four decades. Furthermore, over a hundred young men sensed God's call to the ministry in that church and today are preaching the gospel around the world. Swank had the passion of a preacher who extended the appeal not only where all could publicly see him, but also in the dens and living rooms of the city, out of sight to all but his hearers and his Lord.

Pastors have the immense privilege of calling men and women to the Lord Jesus Christ. The pastor not consistently offering an appeal in person makes himself a hypocrite and will find it exceedingly difficult to offer a public appeal with a passion that will produce lasting fruit.

MAKE YOUR GOSPEL INVITATIONS PLEASANT

Gospel appeals ought to be issued with a winsome smile and pleasant manner. Yet Christians sometimes make the gospel seem offensive because of how they present it to others. Berating or bullying others into a "decision" does not lead to spiritual success. Neither does intimidation nor embarrassment produce lasting commitments. Using undue pressure is not as advantageous as being pleasant.

The Bible records that the early believers who were most successful in one-on-one evangelism had "favor with all the people" (Acts 2:47). They were pleasant in their proclamation and winsome in their witness, and many thousands responded to their public and private appeals in the first few months following the birth of the church in Jerusalem.

Unfortunately, today too few followers of Christ are consistently establishing friendships with unsaved people. In the quest to "go out from their midst, and be separate from them" (2 Cor 6:17), Christians have confused insulation from the world with isolation from the world. However, there is a revealing postscript

added at the end of Luke's moving chapter on the nativity: "And
Jesus increased in wisdom and in stature and in favor with God
and man" (Luke 2:52). Jesus Himself enjoyed a balanced life.
He grew intellectually, physically, spiritually, and socially. He
grew in favor with people. He was gracious and friendly as He
approached others.

Jesus established pleasant relationships everywhere He went
to plead with people to repent and believe, and men and women
were caught up in His warm personality. He established relationships at a well one day and in the marketplace the next. He never
intimidated nor shamed others into becoming His followers. The
church's direst need today is for members to venture outside the
four walls of the sanctuary and touch the lives of those in need
of Christ, and do this winsomely. The public appeals on Sunday
would assume a new spirit of expectancy if the personal appeals
throughout the week were done consistently and pleasantly, in
line with the example of Christ.

In Acts 2:47 the early believers were accepted by the people,
but those within the religious establishment of the day rejected
them. They were a threat to traditional religion, which had
become stale and institutionalized. The Roman government
oppressed Christians for their refusal to bow before Caesar "as
lord," but the people in streets and markets, and in towns and
villages, embraced them. These early believers were effective in
their witness and their worship, and thousands responded to
their appeals to accept Christ. The ministry of Christ and His
followers was so effective because they were not selective in offering their appeals. They were net fishermen casting widely over all
the people—not hook fishermen fishing for only one type of fish.

An idea originating among church-growth gurus teaches
that churches should "target" only a certain group of individuals
on the socioeconomic scale. Followed to the extreme, such techniques are foreign to the New Testament pattern. The Jerusalem

church enjoyed the fellowship of the richest of the rich in Joseph of Arimathea and the poorest of the poor, represented by the widow who gave her all (cf. Luke 21:2–4). Since heaven will host that same variety of people, why should churches be prone to compartmentalize here on earth by race, social standing, or economic status? Thus, pastors must make their appeals in a cordial manner in order to be God-blessed in their witness so they can find favor and gain a hearing with *all* people.

A simple smile can have an unbelievably disarming effect—it can break down a wall of hesitation or build a bridge for a person to cross over the chasm of unbelief. As pastors extend the public appeal, they need not whip or drive their hearers to the altar. Instead, they can step to the side of the pulpit and lovingly call the lost to faith in Christ.

MAKE YOUR GOSPEL INVITATIONS PATIENT

The public appeal is often the most neglected part of the entire worship service. It has been a routine portion of the service for many churches, which associate it with a long-standing tradition and extend it weekly without any expectancy or enthusiasm from those in the pulpit or in the audience. It almost always seems to be "tacked on" at the end of a sermon, usually accompanied by a verse or two of a familiar hymn. This lackadaisical attitude is the very reason the public appeal so often lacks a visible response. On the contrary, the invitation should instead be the culmination of every worship experience.

Since the public appeal presents the perfect opportunity for men and women to act on what they have heard and felt in the service, it should be given patiently, allowing the Holy Spirit time to move the hearts of the hearers and draw them to Christ. It should be carefully thought about, planned for, and prayed over, because it is a vital part of the worship service. Time for giving the appeal should be allotted and protected so the preacher does not undergo the pressure of having to rush through his invitation at the end of the service.

Hurried and haphazard appeals seldom result in a positive response. Those planning the service generally discuss which hymns would be appropriate, what the content of the pastoral prayer will be, how the special music will be arranged, who will give the offertory prayer, who will make the announcements, what subject the sermon will address, and even who will pray the benediction—but the public invitation often goes undiscussed.

Consequently, the appeal is often given no priority and is viewed as an addendum to the sermon. This attitude carries over from pulpit to pew, and the appeal is gradually squeezed into an ineffective couple of minutes. This is unacceptable—if the public appeal is worth doing, it should be done patiently, not hurriedly.

The pastor has a responsibility to instill importance and priority into the public appeal. Those in the pew need to be taught to remain patient, prayerful, and positive during the appeal. For example, if people think it is acceptable to leave through the back doors as the pastor calls people to the front, this distraction will detract from the invitation. The pastor may need to be direct in his instruction to the congregation: *"I am going to ask that not a single person leave this room unless it is an absolute emergency. This is God's time of invitation."*

Pastors must make the invitation a priority by planning for it, praying about it, and giving it the appropriate space, patiently allowing the Holy Spirit time to do His work of conviction of sin and convincing of Christ's righteousness.

MAKE YOUR GOSPEL
INVITATIONS PUBLIC

While the gospel invitation has been effectively used since the days of the New Testament, some object to its having any place in a corporate worship service. Yet Jesus said, "Everyone who acknowledges me before men, I also will acknowledge before my Father who is in heaven" (Matt 10:32). Jesus never called anyone to follow Him outside of a public context. Yes, Nicodemus did come privately to Jesus one night, but Christ always initiated encounters publicly. For instance, He was walking along the shores of the Sea of Galilee and saw a group of fishermen mending their nets. He looked into the faces of Andrew and Peter, along with James and John, and said, "Follow me, and I will make you fishers of men" (4:19). And they did, in front of all their friends and fellow fishermen. They stepped out publicly and followed Jesus.

In Capernaum Jesus encountered Matthew, the tax collector, sitting at the receipt of customs on a busy workday with several customers and clients around. Jesus spoke those two simple words: "Follow me" (9:9). And Matthew did, in front of all those people who knew him best.

When Jesus passed through Jericho, throngs of people lined the streets for a glimpse of Him. Jesus stopped under a tree, looked up, saw Zacchaeus watching, and called for him to come down and walk with Him. And Zacchaeus did, in front of everyone (Luke 19:1–10).

Every time Jesus called men and women to follow Him, He did it publicly. There is something about responding to a public appeal that helps seal this commitment in a person's life. It is simply one of those "tangible intangibles."

In terms of effectiveness in recent history, one name stands alone—Billy Graham. In defending his use of appeals, Graham stated, "Some who are against public evangelistic invitations go to almost any length using the appeal in personal evangelism. If it is right to ask a single sinner to repent and receive the Lord Jesus Christ, why is it not right to ask a whole audience to do the same?"[2] The public appeal goes hand in hand with the personal appeal. It makes no sense to spend thirty minutes explaining the gospel, encouraging the audience toward it, and exhorting them to receive it as a free gift of God's grace, but then dismiss the crowd without ever giving them an opportunity to respond. If it is right to extend the appeal personally and privately, it is equally correct to offer it publicly.

At a graduation exercise not one of the graduates in cap and gown is embarrassed or ashamed to step out publicly, walk to the front of the auditorium, shake the hand of the principal, and receive his or her diploma. In fact, many graduates are cheered on by their family and friends. The same principle applies at a wedding. The bride and groom unashamedly and unapologetically walk down the center aisle of the church to commit their lives to each other in an open and public manner. This public act brings tremendous joy and encouragement to family and friends and simultaneously helps to seal the commitment in the couple's lives. If public appeals are good enough for graduations and weddings, how much more for those making life's greatest commitment to the Lord Jesus Christ?

Most of us identify with something—or someone—we love. For example, people wear sports logos or branded clothing; they carry key chains with automobile insignias; or they wear fraternity pins and school jackets. Likewise, the public appeal gives people the opportunity to identify openly, unashamedly, and publicly with the one whom they now love—the Lord Jesus Christ.

The public appeal has had a significant place in Christian commitment since the Lord used it almost two thousand years ago, and today's pastors need a fresh boldness in their duty to invite the lost to Christ publicly. In fact, Christians cannot expect people to stand for Christ outside the four walls of the church, where the world is indifferent and often hostile to the gospel, if these people have no opportunity to respond publicly before Christians who will rejoice in their decisions for Christ. Pastors, lead your congregation in the face of an uninterested and often antagonistic culture. Publicly give the invitation and see what God will do.

MAKE YOUR GOSPEL INVITATIONS PREMEDITATED

Proper planning and premeditation should not be an afterthought for those who seek to sharpen their skills in publicly presenting the gospel's appeal. After a pastor completes sermon preparation, he should begin to plan and pray about the invitation by asking, "So what?" The appeal should be a vital part of the sermon and issue from it, melting the message into the truth found in Ephesians 2:8–9: "For by grace you have been saved through faith. And this is not your own doing; it is the gift of God, not a result of works, so that no one may boast."

The invitation should make salvation's *outset* plain: where does salvation begin? No one can live a Christian life without a clear understanding of its outset. If Christians are not right at the beginning, they will be wrong everywhere else. Salvation's outset is in these words: "For by grace you have been saved." Salvation is not God's response to a person's good works—it is solely and entirely of grace, God's unmerited favor. The public appeal should also make salvation's *outlet* plain: "You have been saved through faith." Faith is the outlet, the conduit, through which God's grace flows to man's heart. "Without faith it is impossible to please [God]" (Heb 11:6).

One danger during the public appeal occurs when hearers equate the act of "walking down an aisle" or "coming to the front" of an auditorium with the miracle of regeneration itself. Thus, pastors should make plain not only salvation's outset and outlet, but also salvation's *outcry*. The outcry lies in these words: "And this is not your own doing . . . not a result of works, so that no one may boast" (Eph 2:8–9). Eternal salvation is not about a person's work ethic, and every appeal should echo this good news.

Appeals should also be clear regarding salvation's *outlay*. Paul emphasizes that salvation "is the gift of God" (v. 8). Thus, salvation is not a goal to be achieved but a gift to be received. Failure to grasp this simple truth has resulted in all sorts of spiritual errors and given rise to cults and other false religions. Consequently, pastors engaging in the sacred task of issuing the public appeal must differentiate the physical act of responding from the reception of the free gift of God's grace, which comes only through faith.

The highest calling and the greatest privilege in life is introducing men and women to the Lord Jesus Christ, so appeals need to be fully premeditated in order for pastors to extend Christ's call faithfully to receive the gift of eternal life through faith alone and by His grace.

MAKE YOUR GOSPEL INVITATIONS PSYCHOLOGICAL

The scene of an athlete standing on top of the winner's platform at the Olympic Games while his or her national anthem plays forever seals this achievement in his or her mind. In the same way, publicly responding to Christ helps affirm a person's decision in his or her life. Thus, just as in a public wedding ceremony, a winner's platform, or a graduation exercise, the response to the public appeal can be psychologically therapeutic. Human nature encourages us to make responses openly and unashamedly. Even though the word *psychological* is used here, this does not insinuate that pastors should play mind games with their hearers, appealing to them through some sort of mental manipulation. Frankly, people need an outlet—an avenue of response—to affirm their own personal commitment to Jesus Christ to others. The public appeal provides exactly that—it is psychologically beneficial.

When Christians openly and publicly make a spiritual decision, they gain a mental visual aid that lasts a lifetime. Private and personal decisions are often forgotten after a short time, but the response to a public appeal is never forgotten. Here is a helpful analogy: Most pastors can probably share the stories of their calls to full-time ministry. Perhaps a man initially had his own plans for his life, but eventually he began sensing that God had other plans. Eventually he realized that he could find no joy in anything but vocational ministry, but he still wavered back and forth from day to day. That man's resolve was only solidified when he made his calling public. He will never forget the day he stood before his home church and made his decision public—the image is imprinted in his mind. Thus, making a public commitment clearly and psychologically seals a decision forever in a person's heart and mind.

Public appeals are also psychologically stimulating and challenging to those who observe them. For example, pastors can encourage this energy by acknowledging men and women in the church who come with people to the front in the moment of public appeal and lead them to Christ. This causes many others to think, "If Bill or Tom or Mary or Kathy can bring someone to Jesus, then I can too." Also, when children respond to the appeal, pastors can remind their hearers that Jesus encouraged anyone who follows after Him to come like little children in simple childlike faith (cf. Matt 19:14).

Christian psychologists are quick to point out the positive benefits of the public appeal. Impulses to follow Christ will diminish unless they are acted upon quickly. The public appeal gives people an opportunity, in the words of the ancient proverb, "to strike while the iron is hot." Anecdotally, it seems that men and women are less apt to respond the second or third time they hear an appeal. In fact, Paul stated to the Ephesians that the heart becomes harder and more calloused until people reach a point when they can no longer hear God's calls because their hearts are so hardened from repeatedly neglecting Christ's appeal (cf. Eph 4:18–19). The appeal thus contains a psychological urgency strongly encouraging people to respond. *Carpe diem*—"Seize the day!"

This principle holds true in the parlor as well as in the public arena. It is vital for Christians sharing the good news of eternal life to give people the opportunity to let others know of and share in their newfound joy.

MAKE YOUR GOSPEL
INVITATIONS PERPETUAL

One subtle danger about the public appeal is that some people may think it is the best, and perhaps only, forum where people can make a decision for Jesus Christ. For instance, during the twentieth century most every rural church in American held a "protracted" two-week revival in July or August of every year. It was *the* time for unbelievers to "get saved." If certain individuals went through the "protracted meeting" without responding and being converted, church members would comment to one another, "Let's pray and maybe next August he or she will be saved at that time."

On the contrary, the appeal to follow Christ should be *perpetual.* Many churches make a tremendous mistake in thinking the invitation ends when the people leave the church building. The appeal to follow Christ is not merely what the preacher does once or twice a week from the pulpit; rather, it should permeate church ministries and the lifestyles of its members. Quite frankly, many of those who walk forward in church have probably already responded to a personal appeal from a church member who "draws the net" as a way of life in the marketplace day by day.

This appeal to others should saturate everything pastors do, and committees should keep those who are "not here yet" in mind as they make all of the church's decisions. Pastors should also encourage their congregants to build relationships with lost people. After all, Jesus did this. The Lord made personal appeals to those in need wherever He went, whether at a well or in a marketplace. Pastors should thus continue to emphasize the importance of making decisions and planning programs for those who are "not here yet." Many churches make their decisions on the basis of those already there or, worse yet, those who have been there for forty years. Churches will never impact the world with the gospel through public appeals alone; their members must adopt a spirit of evangelism and engage in personal and private appeals as a lifestyle.

Doors of opportunity await opening. Before the end of any worship service, pastors should inform their hearers where they will be available, along with counselors, to meet in order to discuss faith, answer questions, and offer counsel about any decisions that were made during the service.

MAKE YOUR GOSPEL INVITATIONS PRESUMPTIVE

This volume offers many suggestions and variations in how ministers can extend Christ's appeal to others in public settings, but ultimately the minister must be himself. Being *presumptive* means "giving grounds for reasonable opinion or belief." In challenging Christians to make the invitation presumptive, this section clarifies that the appeal should be logical; it should make sense.

A preacher should identify with the interests of the people in wherever God has placed him to advance His kingdom. For example, one young pastor in a rural farming community became notorious for using detailed sermonic illustrations of such things as nuclear fission, genetic engineering, and a host of other subjects which those good and godly farmers did not have a clue about. In contrast to this incorrect approach, the privilege of extending Christ's appeal calls for credibility and common sense. Pastors should exercise their own judgment and be natural, speaking the language of their people and meeting them at the points of their own interests. This consideration will go far in building the foundation for a winsome witness.

Jesus always appealed to an individual at the point of his or her particular interest. To the butcher, He became the "Lamb of God." To the baker, He was the "Bread of Life." To the candlestick maker, He was the "Light of the World." He also appealed to the wise men at the point of their interest; they were astronomers and interested in the study of the stars. What did He do? He caught them with a star that led them to Bethlehem. Most of the disciples were engaged in the fishing business around the Sea of Galilee. The Lord made His public appeal to them by highlighting their chosen trade. He said, "Follow me, and I will make you fishers of men" (Matt 4:19). Later, in Samaria at Jacob's well, He met a woman who had ventured out in the heat because she needed to get water. He made His personal appeal to her by emphasizing her particular need and interest, speaking of "living water" (John 4:10).

Wherever the Lord went, He never tried to become someone or something He was not, but He always adapted His appeal to others according to their particular interests. In the same way, pastors should be themselves while discerning and addressing the needs of those to whom they preach.

MAKE YOUR GOSPEL INVITATIONS PUNCTUAL

Although many effective pastors, evangelists, and ministers of the past have been strong proponents of giving long, extended, and protracted invitations, appeals should still be punctual once the message of redemption has been adequately and persuasively presented. Churches that are winning the greatest numbers to Christ today seldom extend long invitations. There is a discernable difference in today's evangelistic churches and those of the preceding generation, which might have sung nine or ten stanzas of an invitation hymn with no response.

When the men and women of the church are making personal appeals and leading people to faith in Christ during the course of the week, the time of public appeal can be punctual and to the point. The people have already been won and made ready—the pastor can simply preach and watch at the time of invitation as the congregants walk side by side with those whom they personally brought to the Lord.

Some pastors make the mistake of coming to the very moment of "drawing the net" but then taking off on a tangent. They often lose their hearers at this point. This can happen in a time of personal appeal when an unexpected question encourages the speaker to "chase a rabbit." In contrast, effective and lasting appeals are most generally punctual and to the point, avoiding distraction. This focus should not be confused with a robotic and mechanical approach. Rather, punctuality comes from being sensitive to both the Holy Spirit and the responses of hearers. When God is at work and the Spirit is obviously moving, the pastor should keep in tune with His leading and extend the appeal.

MAKE YOUR GOSPEL INVITATIONS PROFICIENT

Quality matters in doing the kingdom's business. Preachers of the gospel should show excellence in all they do, especially in the task of advancing the kingdom of God. Those called to extend the evangelistic appeal should continually strive to sharpen their skills. However, in the economy of God, good is the enemy of the best. Often, every aspect in the worship service is given a quality control check—except the public appeal. In many minds, the invitation is simply a given fixture relegated to its place at the end of the sermon as a sort of "sacred cow," but it is never given creative thought or attention.

Nevertheless, the world outside the church certainly gives attention to closing a deal. Major corporations spend an incredible amount of time and training to teach their sales forces how to do this, and books written in this field strongly emphasize the importance of pressing toward a decision. Salespersons of all kinds and types are well trained in the art of drawing the net in their respective professions. Likewise, ministers already make certain that the music is good quality, the sermon is fine-tuned, and the entire service flows from the "call to worship" to the benediction. But they must also address the quality of the public appeals they offer—this will crown their efforts.

CONCLUSION

Gospel invitations do not embody all the characteristics this chapter mentions to meet an obligatory set of criteria, but instead seek to make Christian disciples. In fishing for people, gospel preachers must not only "cast" or "draw the net," as important as those steps are. Once the "net has been drawn," the task has only begun. Pastors must then retrieve the "fish" from the "net" and "harvest" them.

This "harvesting" involves training and discipleship of new converts so that the churches do not become a mile wide and an inch deep. One of the characteristics of the first church was that their converts "devoted themselves to the apostles' teaching" (Acts 2:42). The preservation of new converts is the proof that an evangelistic appeal has truth and integrity. However, the lack of preservation of new converts exposes not only poor follow-up but often manipulative gospel appeals.

Steps to make the public appeal productive can begin immediately. Two primary reasons for offering a public invitation are (1) to give an opportunity for those who made a personal decision for Christ during the week to acknowledge Him before men (cf. Matt 10:32) and (2) to provide an opportunity to present a personal appeal to those who respond as inquirers. Ministers and trained laypersons can immediately engage with those who come forward, perhaps in a designated welcome center. The church can raise up individuals to serve in this way by offering a course in evangelism that includes systematic theology, Scripture memory, articulation of the faith, and biblical counseling techniques.

Before new converts leave the church building, ministers and laypersons should provide resources for further spiritual development. For example, the church may enroll new believers in a course on the fundamentals of the faith so they can learn to pray, study God's Word, fellowship with others, and follow the other basics of the Christian life.

Pastors should outline steps for making those appeals productive for new believers. The church should seek to bring the new believer into a small Bible study group where he or she can be taught to discover his or her spiritual gifts in order to become an active participant in one of the church's ministries. New converts can set the goal of enrolling in an evangelism training ministry so they learn to articulate their newfound faith as a way of life. Those who are fresh "out of the world" know the most lost people and can have the greatest impact on those most in need of Christ. Indeed, public gospel appeals are not the end but only the beginning of the harvest.

AFTERWORD

WE HAVE NOW COME TO THE END OF A VOLUME THAT WE pray will be the beginning of a new journey for not only you, but also a multitude of pastors and churches. While these pages have been filled with biblical and historical precedents for extending the gospel invitation, accompanied by practical applications, we desire that you leave with a primary awareness that your passion for speaking for Christ comes from prayer and power emerging within you, not from plans or programs engineered from without. Remember that Christ declared His purpose in coming was "to seek and to save the lost" (Luke 19:10). As you stand to share the riches of His gospel, you do not stand before "unreached people groups" or "seekers"—you stand before those who are lost . . . lost beyond hope, beyond time, and beyond eternity!

Your God-given task is not simply to "cast the net" each week, but also to make a priority of "drawing the net." Remember, when the time came for the Lord Jesus to choose His team that would steward His commission to take the gospel to the entire world, He visited neither the universities nor the seats of political power in order to select the brightest and best they had to offer. Instead, Jesus chose rough and quasi-literate fishermen with calloused hands. He knew that a real fisherman was *positive*, because fishermen expect to catch fish every time they lower their nets or bait their hooks. Jesus also knew a real fisherman was *persistent* in trying different methods if a particular net-casting technique or bait was not working. Additionally, a real fisherman was *patient*—for fishermen stay at their task even when the fish are not biting or rushing into the net. Finally, our Lord knew that a fisherman was *passionate*, always hating to lose just one fish. Jesus is still calling us to the task of leading men and women to Him. And He is still looking for those of us who are positive, persistent, patient, and passionate to be His own "fishers of men."

When you finish developing a gospel sermon, you should make a habit of putting down three questions at the end of your sermon notes. First, "What?" What am I trying to say? Did I get the message across? Second, "So What?" Does what I preached really have any pertinent application to the lives of my hearers? Does it have potential to make a difference? Finally, "Now What?" That is, how do I expect my hearers to respond to this message? At this point, you need to consider carefully and develop your transition so that it flows smoothly from the body of the message into the gospel invitation.

We conclude by hoping that a vast number of pastors, preachers, and evangelists might rediscover the prominence and importance of the public pledge, the invitation to trust in Christ. We are never more New Testament in our approach than when we, "with many other words," follow in the steps of Simon Peter by exhorting, pleading, and passionately encouraging those under our hearing to pledge their faith publicly as we extend . . . *The Gospel Invitation.*

CRAFTING THE PUBLIC GOSPEL INVITATION WORKSHEET

Step One: Classify which of the three categorical genres—*Poem, Story,* or *Letter*—best describes the passage of Scripture you will preach.

SELECTED TEXT: _____

GENRE CLASSIFICATION: _____

Step Two: Identify specific ways or cues that the textual idea of the Scripture passage you will preach relates to the gospel.

How Does the Textual Idea Connect with the Gospel?

_____

_____

_____

_____

> **Step Three:** Using the gospel cues identified in *Step Two*, locate and articulate the spiritual needs and/or spiritual problems present in the passage of Scripture you will preach, which only the gospel can solve.

The spiritual needs and/or spiritual problems in this passage that relate to unbelievers include:

_____ (vv. ___).

_____ (vv. ___).

_____ (vv. ___).

_____ (vv. ___).

_____ (vv. ___).

_____ (vv. ___).

> **Step Four:** Contextualize the spiritual needs and/or spiritual problems identified in *Step Three* into *profile descriptions* of unbelievers who will hear you preach this passage of Scripture. Then compose specific *gospel exhortations* by which you or a decision encourager can instruct them how to become baptized, obedient disciples of Jesus Christ. Utilize as many key words as you can from the passage in your articulation of the *profile description* and the *gospel exhortation*.

A. PROFILE DESCRIPTION OF _____:

_____

_____

_____

_____

_____

GOSPEL EXHORTATION:

_____

_____

_____

_____

_____

B. PROFILE DESCRIPTION OF _____:

_____

_____

_____

_____

_____

GOSPEL EXHORTATION:

_____

_____

_____

_____

_____

C. PROFILE DESCRIPTION OF _____:

_____

_____

_____

_____

_____

GOSPEL EXHORTATION:

_____
_____
_____
_____
_____

D. PROFILE DESCRIPTION OF _____:

_____
_____
_____
_____
_____

GOSPEL EXHORTATION:

_____
_____
_____
_____
_____

E. PROFILE DESCRIPTION OF _____:

_____
_____
_____
_____

GOSPEL EXHORTATION:

_____
_____
_____
_____

F. PROFILE DESCRIPTION OF _____:

_____

_____

_____

_____

_____

GOSPEL EXHORTATION:

_____

_____

_____

_____

_____

G. PROFILE DESCRIPTION OF _____:

_____

_____

_____

_____

_____

GOSPEL EXHORTATION:

_____

_____

_____

_____

_____

APPENDIX 2

AN EXAMPLE OF A
PUBLIC GOSPEL APPEAL

THE PRIMARY INTENT OF THE PUBLIC APPEAL IS TO GIVE THOSE who hear the gospel—that is, Jesus's death, burial, and resurrection for their sins—an opportunity to repent of their sins and believe in Christ alone for their salvation, in order that they can become His baptized, obedient disciples. The appeal encourages each inquirer to respond positively and speak with a trained decision encourager in the "welcome center" immediately following the public appeal. Once the message concludes and the transition to the appeal is made, the scene is set. The congregation remains seated with bowed heads, and the pastor initiates the appeal.

The following script is a word-by-word example of a public appeal that O. S. Hawkins might have preached on any given Sunday, as he did weekly in both the First Baptist Church of Fort Lauderdale, Florida, and the First Baptist Church in Dallas, Texas:

In just a moment I am going to ask you to do something that is going to take courage. I am going to ask you to leave your seat, step into the aisle, make your way to the front, and join

138

me here for a prayer. Many of you are going to come to be included in this prayer this morning. Some of you have never opened your heart's door to receive the free gift of eternal life, Jesus Christ, as your very own personal Savior. You have a divine appointment with Him this morning, and you are not here by accident.

Perhaps you sense God's Spirit knocking at the door of your heart, but quite honestly, you just don't know what you would say if you were to respond and join me here at the front. I have good news for you. You do not have to worry about what to say. By your coming you will be saying, "I am going to go God's way today!" When you get here, I am going to lead us all in a word of prayer. We have some Bible study material to give you to help you, and if you come as an inquirer we want the privilege of leading you to faith in the Lord Jesus. Your trusting in Him alone this morning means that God will forgive you of all your sin and make it just as if it never had happened. It also means that Christ Himself will take up residence in your life and never leave you. It means He will give you a place in heaven and a heavenly time on the way. So, in just a moment, I am going to ask you to come and receive this free gift.

There are others of you here this morning who have already opened your hearts to Christ; perhaps this week, last week, last month, or whenever. But you have never stood for Him publicly, openly, or unashamedly. In just a moment, I am going to ask you to join the others who are coming. By your coming to be included in this prayer, you will be saying, "I am making a public pledge of my life to Jesus Christ." There is something about this pledge that will help seal it in your life. After all, our Lord never called anyone to follow Him outside of a public context. At the seaside He called the fishermen to follow Him in front of all their business associates and friends. In Jericho He called Zacchaeus to follow Him in front of the huge crowd lining the street. So there is just something about publicly standing for Christ that helps seal the personal decision that has already been made in our hearts. In fact, Jesus said, "So everyone who acknowledges me before men, I also will acknowledge before my Father who is in heaven" (Matt 10:32). How can you expect to stand for Christ in the marketplaces of the world, which are so hostile to Him, if you will not stand for Him by walking down a carpeted aisle of an air-conditioned church in front of a lot of Christians who will rejoice with you in your decision? Therefore, in a moment when others come I am going to ask you to lead the way to this altar.

Still others of you are here who are Christians but not active in a local church in our city. Perhaps you have just moved here. You have moved everything you have—your furniture, your family, and even your pets. Everything, that is, except your church membership. In a moment I am going to ask you to join the others in coming, and by doing so you will be saying, "I am going to come out of the shadows today and put on the uniform of church membership and serve Christ in and through this local expression of His body." You have been eating your spiritual food here for some time. You have been thinking about joining our team. You have even been planning on it and praying about it. The only thing left is to do it right now. By your coming to join us this morning and being included in this prayer, you will also be serving as an escort for many here who personally need to know Jesus Christ.

There are yet others of you here this morning with a friend who needs to know Jesus. Perhaps the Spirit of God would have you reach out and take that friend by the hand and say, "Let's go God's way this morning. I'll go with you. Let's go together!" Many people in the Bible did this very thing.

Andrew found Peter, took him by the hand, and brought him to Jesus. Philip brought Nathanael. And on and on the church has grown. You can be confident that if the Spirit is leading you to encourage your friend, He is dealing with his heart at the same time. He leads a Philip to the Gaza desert because He is working on the heart of an Ethiopian and wants Philip to take him by the hand and bring him to Jesus. He leads a Peter to Caesarea because He is simultaneously working on the heart of a Cornelius. So, take your friend by the hand this morning and say, "Let's go together. I'll go with you." Bring your friend to Jesus. You will be so glad you did.

Some of you are here this morning and are honest enough to say, "Preacher, I don't know what I need. But my life has no purpose, peace, or direction." That something which you've been searching for to fill the void of life can be found this morning in Someone, and His sweet name is the Lord Jesus. I am going to ask you to join the others in coming to be included in this prayer. Don't worry about what to say when you get here. By your coming as an inquirer you will be saying, "I want to go God's way today and trust in Him." Thus, when you come, "Your sins He'll wash away, your night He'll turn to day, your life . . . He'll make it over anew." He has a brand-new life for you and a brand-new beginning!

Whatever the decision may be in your heart—to know Christ personally, to pledge your life publicly to Him, to unite with our fellowship and join our team, to bring a friend to Jesus, or simply to come in honest inquiry—I am going to ask you to leave your seat, make your way to the front, and join me here. By your coming you are saying, "I am going God's way today." Don't wait for anyone else. If you feel the slightest tugging at your heartstrings, it is the Spirit of God. Many are going to come, and it is the right thing to do. You lead the way, right now!

At this point in the public appeal, the congregation remains seated in a spirit of prayer while men and women, along with boys and girls, respond to the appeal. Times often occur when, as the Spirit directs, the appeal is generally extended in one of the following ways using the Word of God:

The Bible says, "Today, if you hear his voice, do not harden your hearts" (Heb 3:7–8, 15; 4:7). I am speaking finally and fleetingly to those of you here who "hear his voice" in your heart. You will know it if this happens. It is as if He is knocking at your heart's door and pulling at your heartstrings. Every time He calls and you refuse, your heart gets a little harder. In fact, the word the Bible uses to describe this is "callous" (Eph 4:19). If you have had a callus on your hands or feet, you are aware that you can stick a pin in it and never feel it. Continually refusing Christ's call has the same effect on your heart. A time may come when, even though He is still calling, you no longer will hear Him. That is why this hour is urgent. If you perceive the slightest feeling in your heart that God is calling you to Himself, come now. Yes, "today, if you hear his voice, do not harden your heart."

The Bible says, "Seek the LORD while he may be found; call upon him while he is near" (Isa 55:6). He is waiting for you this morning. He is very near your heart. Yes, Jesus is passing by your heart this very moment. Some of you are closer to coming to Him than you have been in a lifetime. You may never be this close again. Seize the moment. He will meet you like the father met his prodigal son, with open arms, no pointed fingers, or clenched fists—just wide-open arms which say, "Come."

The Bible says, "The Spirit himself bears witness with our spirit that we are children of God" (Rom 8:16). Perhaps you are uncertain of your eternal destiny. Bow your head and ask yourself this question: "Am I saved?" Does the Holy Spirit bear witness with your spirit? The Bible also says, "For all who are led by the Spirit of God are sons of God" (v. 14). What is the Holy Spirit leading you to do this morning? Think about it.

If you are without Christ, what do you think He is leading you to do? He will not lead you to walk out those back doors in rejection or neglect. If you have placed your trust in Him but never let anyone know it, what do you suppose He is leading you to do right now? To walk out and continue being a secret disciple? Or to join us at this altar in an open pledge of your life to the One who stood for you in life, through death, and to life again?

If you are not active in a local church, what do you suppose Jesus is leading you to do? Soldiers in the United States Army are not just a part of a worldwide endeavor; they are assigned to a local base where they are accountable and are given assignments of service. The same holds true in God's army; He assigns us to local bases, and perhaps He is assigning you here today.

If you are with a friend who needs to know Jesus, what do you suppose Jesus is leading you to do? Encourage your friend toward Christ or walk out without a word?

Yes, those who are led by the Spirit of God are sons (and daughters) of God. God, the Holy Spirit, is leading you this morning to the Lord Jesus Christ, and by your coming to join these many others already here, you will be indicating you are going God's way today. And it is the right thing to do. I will meet you as you come.

NOTES

CHAPTER 1: PUBLIC INVITATIONS IN THE BIBLE

1. Roy Fish, *Coming to Jesus: Giving a Good Invitation* (North Charleston, SC: CreateSpace, 2015), 3.

CHAPTER 2: THE NECESSITY OF PUBLIC GOSPEL INVITATIONS

1. C. E. Autrey concurred with this sentiment and made practical application of it when he wrote:

> Peter was very much under the direction of the Holy Spirit while he exhorted when he preached. The evangelist is not pushing the Holy Spirit aside when he pleads in the invitation any more than when he prepares and delivers the body of the sermon. He does brush the Holy Spirit aside if he resorts to tricks and traps by which he seeks to pressure the audience into a premature decision. The honest preacher will use the invitation to help [people] decide for God, but he will not ensnare the people into moves which are unreal and are products of fleshly agitation. The evangelistic invitation is a form of persuasion, but it is persuasion carefully guarded by the Holy Spirit. The evangelist[ic preacher] must ever remain mindful that he is persuading [people] in the power of the Holy Spirit to accept Christ as Savior (*Basic Evangelism* [Grand Rapids: Zondervan, 1959], 128–129).

2. John B. Polhill, *Acts*, The New American Commentary 26 (Nashville: Broadman & Holman Publishers, 1992), 355.
3. Jonathan T. Pennington, *Small Preaching: 25 Little Things You Can Do Now to Become a Better Preacher* (Bellingham, WA: Lexham Press, 2021), 29; emphasis original.
4. C. H. Dodd, *The Apostolic Preaching and Its Developments* (London: Hodder & Stoughton, 1936; reprint, Grand Rapids: Baker, 1980), 7–8.
5. Michael Green, *Evangelism in the Early Church* (London: Hodder and Stoughton, 1970), 151; emphasis original.
6. Roy Fish, *Giving a Good Invitation* (Nashville: Broadman Press, 1974), 5.

7. John Piper, *The Supremacy of God in Preaching*, rev. ed. (Grand Rapids: Baker, 2004), 96.

8. L. R. Scarborough, *With Christ, After the Lost: A Search for Souls* (Nashville: Sunday School Board, Southern Baptist Convention, 1919), 129.

9. Colin Brown, ed., *New International Dictionary of New Testament Theology*, vol. 1 (Grand Rapids: Zondervan, 1986), 567.

10. J. Josh Smith, *Preaching for a Verdict: Recovering the Role of Exhortation* (Nashville: B&H Academic, 2019), 4–5.

11. R. Alan Streett, *The Effective Invitation: A Practical Guide for the Pastor* (Grand Rapids: Kregel, 1984), 55–130.

12. David Bennett, *The Altar Call: Its Origins and Present Usage* (Lanham, MD: University Press of America, 2000), 103.

13. E. Glenn Hinson, *The Early Church: Origins to the Dawn of the Middle Ages* (Nashville: Abingdon Press, 1996), 63–64.

14. Green, *Evangelism in the Early Church*, 198.

15. E. Glenn Hinson, *The Evangelization of the Roman Empire: Identity and Adaptability* (Macon, GA: Mercer University Press, 1981), 74.

16. Hinson, *The Evangelization of the Roman Empire*, 76.

17. Hinson, *The Evangelization of the Roman Empire*, 272–73.

18. Fish, *Giving a Good Invitation*, 14–15.

19. David Larsen, *The Evangelism Mandate: Recovering the Centrality of Gospel Preaching* (Grand Rapids: Kregel, 1992), 61.

20. Larsen, *The Evangelism Mandate*, 61.

21. D. Martyn Lloyd-Jones, *Knowing the Times: Addresses Delivered on Various Occasions, 1942–77* (Edinburgh: Banner of Truth, 1989), 102.

22. Bennett, *The Altar Call*, 29. In fact, Bennett asserted, "Though an ardent advocate of [the] 'new measures,' and innovations generally, [Finney] was the originator of few, if any, of them. With regard to the altar call, as has been seen, he was not the first to use it, nor the first to develop a theology that would allow for it, nor even the first to form it into a system" (Bennett, *The Altar Call*, 103).

23. See Joseph Tracy, *The Great Awakening* (Boston: Charles Tappan, 1845), 216; R. T. Kendall, *Stand Up and Be Counted* (London: Hodder and Stoughton, 1984), 47; Streett, *The Effective Invitation*, 94; and Fish, *Coming to Jesus*, 13–14; emphasis added.

24. William L. Lumpkin, *Baptist Foundations in the South: Tracing through the Separates the Influence of the Great Awakening, 1754–1787* (Eugene, OR: Wipf & Stock, 2006), 56.

25. See Bennett, *The Altar Call*, 1–22.

26. Jonathan Edwards, "Great Guilt No Obstacle to the Pardon of the Returning Sinner" in *The Works of Jonathan Edwards*, ed. Edward

Hickman (Edinburgh: Banner of Truth, 1974), 2:112; emphasis original.

27. Jonathan Edwards, *A Narrative of Many Surprising Conversions in Northampton and Vicinity, Written in 1736* (Worcester, MA: Moses W. Grout, 1832), 18–19; emphasis added.

28. Nathan Finn, "Some Thoughts on Altar Calls," *Between the Times* (blog), April 10, 2013, https://web.archive.org/web /20210925220300/https://betweenthetimes.sebts.edu/index .php/2013/04/10/some-thoughts-on-altar-calls/.

CHAPTER 3: PLANNING PUBLIC GOSPEL INVITATIONS

1. R. Scott Pace, *Preaching by the Book: Developing and Delivering Text-Driven Sermons* (Nashville: B&H Academic, 2018), 98.

2. D. Martyn Lloyd-Jones, *Preaching & Preachers* (Grand Rapids: Zondervan, 1971), 273–274.

3. Steven Smith, *Recapturing the Voice of God: Shaping Sermons like Scripture* (Nashville: B&H Academic, 2015), 27.

4. Smith, *Recapturing the Voice of God*, 33; emphasis original.

5. Smith, *Recapturing the Voice of God*, 231.

6. J. Josh Smith, *Preaching for a Verdict: Recovering the Role of Exhortation* (Nashville: B&H Academic, 2019), 105–6.

7. Daniel L. Akin, "Applying a Text-Driven Sermon," in *Text-Driven Preaching: God's Word at the Heart of Every Sermon*, ed. Daniel L. Akin, David L. Allen, and Ned L. Mathews (Nashville: B&H Academic, 2010), 284.

CHAPTER 4: EXTENDING PUBLIC GOSPEL INVITATIONS

1. Ray R. Morawski, *Leading People to Christ: Biblical Principles and Helpful Instructions for Personal Evangelism* (Santa Maria, CA: Xulon, 2010), 7.

CHAPTER 5: BEST PRACTICES IN ISSUING PUBLIC GOSPEL INVITATIONS

1. C. H. Spurgeon, "The Royal Savior" (sermon, Metropolitan Tabernacle, London, February 1, 1872), Christian Classics Ethereal Library, https://ccel.org/ccel/spurgeon/sermons56/sermons56.lii .html.

2. Billy Graham, *Biblical Invitations* (Minneapolis: Billy Graham Evangelistic Association, n.d.), 18–19.